AF754471

The Love of Analog

ALSO AVAILABLE FROM BLOOMSBURY:

Introducing Aesthetics and the Philosophy of Art, by Darren Hudson Hick

The Aesthetics and Ethics of Copying, edited by Darren Hudson Hick and Reinold Schmücker

The Love of Analog

Meditations on Value

Darren Hudson Hick

BLOOMSBURY ACADEMIC
LONDON • NEW YORK • OXFORD • NEW DELHI • SYDNEY

BLOOMSBURY ACADEMIC
Bloomsbury Publishing Plc, 50 Bedford Square, London, WC1B 3DP, UK
Bloomsbury Publishing Inc, 1359 Broadway, New York, NY 10018, USA
Bloomsbury Publishing Ireland, 29 Earlsfort Terrace, Dublin 2, D02 AY28, Ireland

BLOOMSBURY, BLOOMSBURY ACADEMIC and the Diana logo are trademarks of Bloomsbury Publishing Plc

First published in Great Britain 2026

Copyright © Darren Hudson Hick, 2026

Darren Hudson Hick has asserted their right under the Copyright, Designs and Patents Act, 1988, to be identified as Author of this work.

Illustrations by the author, Copyright © Darren Hudson Hick, 2026

For legal purposes the Acknowledgments on p. 141 constitute an extension of this copyright page.

Cover design by Matt Thame © Studio Auto
Cover image: vsviridova/Getty Images

All rights reserved. No part of this publication may be: i) reproduced or transmitted in any form, electronic or mechanical, including photocopying, recording or by means of any information storage or retrieval system without prior permission in writing from the publishers; or ii) used or reproduced in any way for the training, development or operation of artificial intelligence (AI) technologies, including generative AI technologies. The rights holders expressly reserve this publication from the text and data mining exception as per Article 4(3) of the Digital Single Market Directive (EU) 2019/790.

Bloomsbury Publishing Inc does not have any control over, or responsibility for, any third-party websites referred to or in this book. All internet addresses given in this book were correct at the time of going to press. The author and publisher regret any inconvenience caused if addresses have changed or sites have ceased to exist, but can accept no responsibility for any such changes.

A catalogue record for this book is available from the British Library.

Library of Congress Cataloging-in-Publication Data

Names: Hick, Darren Hudson author
Title: The love of analog / Darren Hudson Hick.
Description: New York : Bloomsbury Academic, 2026. | Includes bibliographical references and index. | Summary: "There is a culture of analog. Examining the values of analog means examining the meaningful activities of the participants in that culture"– Provided by publisher.

Identifiers: LCCN 2025050706 (print) | LCCN 2025050707 (ebook) | ISBN 9781350612938 HB | ISBN 9781350612945 PB | ISBN 9781350612952 ePDF | ISBN 9781350612969 eBook
Subjects: LCSH: Values | Agent (Philosophy) | Art–Philosophy | Digital media–Social aspects | Technology–Philosophy
Classification: LCC BD435 .H553 2026 (print) | LCC BD435 (ebook)
LC record available at https://lccn.loc.gov/2025050706
LC ebook record available at https://lccn.loc.gov/2025050707

ISBN: HB: 978-1-3506-1293-8
PB: 978-1-3506-1294-5
ePDF: 978-1-3506-1295-2
eBook: 978-1-3506-1296-9

Typeset by RefineCatch Limited, Bungay, Suffolk
Printed and bound in Great Britain

For product safety related questions contact productsafety@bloomsbury.com.

To find out more about our authors and books visit www.bloomsbury.com and sign up for our newsletters.

For Delaina

Contents

Figures

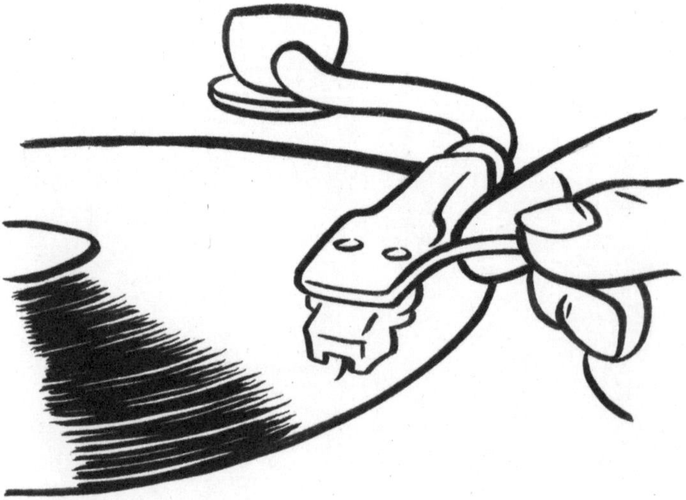

1

The Return to Analog

Being Human

This book is about being human. More specifically, it's about being human in the world we live in. It's about finding out what matters to us. Being human means telling stories, and every story has a beginning. This one starts a few years ago.

My wife, Delaina, and I were on Spring Break when the world shut down in March of 2020. We had taken a day trip to the Columbia Museum of Art and were happily exploring the near-empty complex. Delaina was playing with one of the museum's interactive displays, sliding cubes representing items like a Victorian dress, a molded plastic chair, and Marcel Duchamp's *Bicycle Wheel* into slots designated for stuff that *is* art, stuff that *isn't* art, and stuff that *might* be art.* There wasn't another patron

*For the record, Delaina judged the dress to be art, the chair not-art, and Duchamp's readymade maybe-art.

in sight. But, as soon as we stepped away from the display, museum workers swept in, collected all the blocks, and took them away. Three days later, the museum locked its doors and pivoted entirely to online content. So did we all. Faculty at my school were informed by email that Spring Break would be extended by another week to give us time to convert all of our classes to online instruction. On-campus activities were effectively cancelled until early June, though (we were told) the situation remained fluid. In fact, I wouldn't return to the classroom for another year and a half.

I transitioned pretty smoothly to online teaching. I was already fairly tech-savvy, and I quickly converted our back room into a little studio where I crunched out YouTube lectures, layering audio over PowerPoints, staying just a couple of weeks ahead of my students and my revised syllabus. But I noticed something curious even in those early weeks of lockdown. Whenever I emerged bleary-eyed from my makeshift studio at the end of the day, I would usually mix a couple of cocktails, put on a record, and sit down with Delaina to poke away at a jigsaw puzzle or play a board game. We had small collections of vinyl records, puzzles, and games, and these collections began growing quickly. We sought out yard sales, bought used games over Facebook Marketplace, and started trading jigsaw puzzles with our neighbors. As in-person meetings were replaced with Zoom meetings, and happy hours with friends were replaced with . . . Zoom meetings, analog media became a refuge from the screen. And not just for me. Vinyl record sales and board game sales reached new heights during the pandemic. But lockdown only represented the wide end of a wedge that had been expanding for years. Analog was booming.

By the time that the file-sharing service Napster launched in 1999, vinyl album sales in the US were floating around 1.4 million units a year (down from the glory days of 300+ million in the 1970s), and CD sales were near their peak, just shy of 940 million units.[1] But that changed as consumers began giving up physical media altogether. Napster folded in 2001, the same year that Apple released its first iPod and the iTunes app. The future was becoming clear. CD sales started a downward slide. By 2006, the year that Spotify launched, CD sales were down by a third. By 2009, those sales were cut in half again. But right around the same time, something curious was happening with vinyl. In 2006, less than a million vinyl records were sold in the US. By 2009, it was two and a half million. By 2012, 4.6 million. Between 2019 and 2020, at the start of the pandemic, vinyl sales jumped from 16.8 million to 27.5 million, and again to 41.7 million in 2021. In 2024, US sales hit 43.6 million units, the eighteenth year of consecutive growth, a pattern repeated in the UK and elsewhere.[2] It wasn't just vinyl. Board game sales worldwide jumped 50% in 2020, but were already on a steady upward trend.[3] And, at the same time that big-box book retailers like Borders and Barnes & Noble were shuttering stores and shifting to online sales, independent bookstores were thriving, nearly doubling their numbers in the US between 2009 and 2022.[4]

Personally, I seemed to be seeking out analog in a digital world like someone low on vitamin C craving a tall glass of orange juice without knowing why. And I wanted to know why. While I had always had a foot planted firmly in physical media, my growing collections of records and board games were something new. I was not your typical hipster, eschewing all digital media, stockpiling typewriter ribbons and mustache wax. I wasn't *rejecting* the digital in favor of the analog, but I was definitely supplementing my diet, and consumer trends suggested I wasn't alone. Certainly, someone might suggest that at least some of the increase in record and board game sales (to say nothing of the resurgence of analog photography) is due to nostalgia for these older, more quaint forms of media. And that might certainly be true for some people, but I didn't really grow up with music. My parents owned a few records (at least a quarter of which, I recall, were from the *Hooked on Classics* series), but they didn't play them. A box of 8-tracks was similarly ignored. Somewhere in a closet we had copies of *Monopoly*, *Payday*, and *Mastermind*, but they mostly gathered dust. The games that Delaina and I now own bear little resemblance to these classics, and most of the records we seek out are in genres I didn't previously know existed.[*] The kids buying Taylor Swift and Beyoncé records today were mostly born in the twenty-first century, when vinyl record sales were in the basement, but they represent the biggest surge in vinyl sales. Gen Zers might first encounter new music on TikTok, but they seek it out on vinyl at a rate 27% higher than the average consumer.[5] By one count, just under half of board game enthusiasts are between 18 and 34 years old, having never known a world without video games. So, what is the appeal of analog in this digital age? What was this itch that I was trying to scratch?

---

[*]Particularly early 1960s audiophile lounge jazz.

"Analog"

A quick note of clarification. Throughout this book, I am going to use the term "analog" in a familiar but technically inaccurate way. The analog/digital distinction comes from early computer science, and was used to distinguish two ways of representing things. "Analog" devices represent measures of one thing by way of another thing. The clock in my kitchen is an analog clock: the double-A battery provides a continual flow of energy, which the little motor uses to continually move the hands around. A typical electric guitar is an analog device, too, using electromagnets to sense the vibrations of the strings, generating an electrical signal, which is sent through an amplifier to the speaker to make sounds. "Digital" devices, by contrast, deal with *counts* of things rather than flowing *measures* (we get the word "digital" from our *digits*—our fingers, which we can use to count things): input is converted into discrete numbers (whether 0 through 9, or the binary ones and zeros used in most computers today), which can then be used in all manner of ways. In a nutshell, if it's measures of one thing being directly translated into measures of another, it's analog; if there's a step where input is first converted into some discrete numbers, it's digital. Now, that's all well and good for engineers,* but "analog" tends to be contrasted these days with "digital" in about the same way that "acoustic" came to be

*And some philosophers. The technical analog/digital distinction, particularly as it relates to representation, is the subject of some philosophical debate, including entries by John Haugeland (1981), Nelson Goodman (1968), David Lewis (1971), and John Kulvicki (2015, 2017).

contrasted with "electric" when it came to musical instruments, and I'm going to use "analog" to refer to anything for which there is now a digital equivalent: games, books, photographs, music, and so on.*

Ellul and Efficiency

At least part of my curiosity about the resurgence of analog media—both personally and generally—comes from the observation that analog stuff has all manner of things working against it. Compared with its digital counterparts, analog stuff is expensive, heavy, laborious, persnickety, and notoriously fragile. If I want Taylor Swift's album, *The Tortured Poets Department*, on vinyl, it will run me about $40. It's a two-record album, and weighs a pound and a half. If I want to listen to it, I'll have to have a working turntable nearby. After every four songs, I'll have to get up and flip the record. If I don't store it in its case, it's likely to attract dust, which will make it sound fuzzy when I play it. It's likely to attract dust anyway, so I'll have to lightly clean it on occasion. I'll have to store it upright, or it's liable to warp, making it unplayable. And if I happen to scratch the soft plastic surface with a fingernail while flipping it, putting it away, or cleaning it, it will be a pound and a half of trash. Alternatively, I

*A little ironically, then, while we tend to think of "analog" things as being more hands-on, and "digital" as more technological, "analog" starts out as a term of technology, and "digital" referred to the most hands-on things of all: our fingers.

can just use my YouTube Premium account, which lets me listen to all the music I want—including every one of Taylor Swift's albums—whenever I want, so long as there's Wi-Fi in the air. All I have to do is tap the screen on any one of my digital devices a couple of times. By comparison, as a reliable means of getting Taylor Swift into my ear, the analog option seems wildly inefficient.

In his 1954 opus, *The Technological Society*, philosopher Jacques Ellul introduced what has come to be known as "the efficiency principle"—the notion that efficiency is the "fixed end" in technology—what all of technology aims at.[6] That is, the end of technology is to get us to *our* ends, whatever they may be, most efficiently.* Efficiency as a value may even begin to overshadow the ends that we were originally trying to reach. Certainly, efficiency is used to *sell* technology. Whatever the product, we're told, the newest technology puts it a step ahead of the competition. A 1979 magazine ad for Air France declares, "Efficiency is the first quality of Concorde. You arrive at your destination twice as fast and thus increase your own efficiency because you are more available."† Enough people, it seems, thought it was worth spending six times as much for a roundtrip ticket across the Atlantic in surprisingly cramped seats if it got

---

*Ellul didn't think this was a good thing. He argues that the prioritization of efficiency runs counter to the "deepest instinct of humankind"—human freedom. See Ellul, *The Technological Society*.

†Perhaps it rolls off the tongue more fluidly in French. The original ad reads, "L'efficacité est la première qualité de Concorde. Vous arrivez à destination deux fois plus vite et augmentiez ainsi votre propre efficacité car vous êtes plus disponible." English translation, appropriately enough, by artificial intelligence.

you there in half the time—enough to keep the Concorde in the air for nearly 30 years.*

The digital realm has always taken efficiency as a primary value. In computer programming, efficiency is essential. Ada Lovelace knew this in 1843, when she offered this observation:†

> In almost every computation a great *variety* of arrangements for the succession of the processes is possible, and various considerations must influence the selection amongst them for the purposes of a Calculating Engine. One essential object is to choose that arrangement which shall tend to reduce to a minimum the *time* necessary for completing the calculation.[7]

That is, there are *lots* of ways to get a computer to do what you want it to do. A better program is an efficient program. A program with fewer lines of code gets the job done faster, and demands fewer resources to run. A program that demands the least of the user offers the most efficient user experience. In this sense, artificial intelligence promises to be the apogee of efficiency, allowing the user to skip right over the means and get directly to the end. In her 2008 book, *The Mantra of Efficiency*, Jennifer Karns Alexander notes how "efficiency" evolved from an abstract philosophical concept tied to creation and causation in the

*A disastrous Air France crash in 2000—the first fatal Concorde crash in history—grounded the airliner. Efficiency assumes that you will actually survive the trip.

†The observation is one of several "Notes" that Lovelace made as the translator of Luigi Menebrea's "Sketch of the Analytical Engine Invented by Charles Babbage." Lovelace's "Notes" are twice as long as Menebrea's own article, and substantially more technical. Note G is generally regarded as containing the world's first computer program.

seventeenth century, to a principle of engineering in the nineteenth, to a more morally laden (if less clear) concept today: "Efficiency became promiscuous, describing activities of all sorts, including marriage, fuel consumption, use of leisure time, and political and moral behavior."[8] Delaina, it must be said, is often concerned that she isn't making the most efficient use of her down time.

At least at first glance, digital media *does* seem entirely guided by the value of efficiency. The *faster* that I can communicate with colleagues around the globe, or design a poster, or access entertainment, the better. Analog media, by contrast, is striking in its inefficient use of time, resources, energy, and space. If, as Jennifer Karns Alexander notes, efficiency has become "an apparently self-evident value" in our culture, what, I wondered, were the values that were driving us to seek out things that are *inefficient* in so many ways?[9]

Pragmatism and Value Pluralism

In philosophy, the study of values is *axiology*, which tends to fold in ethics and aesthetics, as well as such value-laden areas as philosophy of religion and political philosophy. For quite a long time, philosophers have sought what are called *intrinsic values*—those things that are valuable in and of themselves, and that give other things (including other values) their worth. Intrinsic values, typically understood, are independent of human valuing. That is, we value them *because* they are valuable. As such, it doesn't make much sense to ask *why* they are valuable, as that would assume that something *else* (a *more* intrinsic value?) makes them valuable. Rather, intrinsic values would be what Jennifer Karns Alexander calls "self-evident values."

But, if efficiency *was* an intrinsic value, it wouldn't make a lot of sense for us to *forego* its value in favor of such inefficient things as vinyl records, board games, and analog film, unless there was some *other* value or values to be had in such things that were lacking in their digital equivalents. This sort of thinking opens the door to the notion of *value pluralism*—the idea that there are *many* values which cannot simply be cashed out in terms of some single, intrinsic base value. On this view, individual values will be incommensurable: no amount of one will get you the other. Value pluralism is the view embraced by the branch of philosophy called *pragmatism*.

Pragmatism is grounded in the work of three American philosophers: John Dewey, Charles Sanders Peirce, and William James. Since its founding at the turn of the twentieth century, Pragmatism has grown into a broad philosophical tradition challenging the more familiar "analytic" and "Continental" traditions that have largely dominated Western philosophy. Pragmatism is grounded in a number of core tenets, most centrally that knowledge of the world requires acting in it. It is a staunchly empirical philosophy, and grounds its principles in what is observable—including values.

Sometimes we value something because it gets us something else, so the first thing (the means) is *instrumentally* valuable to the second (the end). But, Dewey contends, what counts as a means and what counts as an end depends on what *we* value—how a thing fits into our big picture—and that big picture can change. There are no *means* or *ends* "per se": every end can be a means, and every means an end. Indeed, *being* a means does not stop something from also being *at the same time* an end—a thing valued in itself. Take *happiness* for example, often touted as *the* intrinsic value, both by philosophical hedonists, and by my intro philosophy students. If all that we ultimately value is happiness, then everything that we value, we value for its ability to bring us happiness. I have no doubt that money brings me happiness. And I have no doubt that my marriage brings me happiness. But there is something repulsive in the idea that there *should* be enough money to make me give up on love or family. Perhaps I *do* value my marriage in part because it brings me happiness, but the marriage is not simply exchangeable with other happiness-bearing things. As Dewey puts it, "the relational character of the *things* that are employed as means does not prevent the things from having their own immediate qualities."[10] I value *the marriage itself.*

If you want to know about value, the pragmatist says, look at your life, look at how you need *variety.* When you have to choose between, say, a budding romance and a new job in another state, there is no obvious answer—we can't simply reduce to a common denominator like happiness to make the decision. No matter the trade-in, there will always be a loss. That's why choices are hard.

The pragmatist approach is also one of specifics. That is, the pragmatist will say, talking about values in the abstract is at best difficult because our values will always be more clearly grounded in our specific activities and choices: what do I get out of doing *this*? As such, pragmatism demands a bottom-up rather than top-down approach to values. Rather than looking for absolute values in the abstract realm, in Plato's ether, we should look for values in our *acts of valuing*. Anthony Weston says, if you ask why I climb mountains, I can't capture the truth in saying "it makes me happy"—that is, by pointing to some intrinsic value that settles the matter. Things aren't going to be so simple. "To explain why I climb mountains may take hours," Weston says, "but it is not an endless task: although the story has no final stopping point or ultimate appeal, it is *complete* when I have articulated the manifold connections between mountain climbing and the other values, beliefs, etc. which make up my self."[11]

The sort of values I will be discussing in this book are what might broadly be called "everyday values"—things that tend to go unexplained and overlooked. Much of the philosophical discussion of "value pluralism" focuses on *moral* values or *political* values. The sort of values I will be discussing are neither overtly moral nor overtly political, though I would suggest that our values are such that they will tend to refuse being pigeonholed. What we value in our day-to-day lives will tend to be what we value in our moral and political lives. On that same point, our values tend to interact with each other in interesting and robust ways, so my attempt to separate these notable values into discrete chapters is at best abstract—something that will grate on the pragmatist.*

---

*As pragmatism is grounded in the empirical, abstraction will make the pragmatist itchy. For several reasons, I am not all-in on pragmatism. But the value pluralism embraced by pragmatism has a definite appeal. If we want to talk about values, we should look at what we value.

The pragmatist approach deals as much as it can with particulars, rather than abstracts—a bit of a challenge when you're talking about things like values. So, rather than asking about my values more generally, we have to look at what I value about *this* case, *this* activity, *this* thing, which means I'm going to be doing a lot of storytelling. That being said, while the nature of the pragmatist line is that I can really only examine my own values, I can certainly look around at trends that suggest others might hold these values, too. Although Dewey suggests that our individual values can change regularly, other pragmatists note that since at least some of our valuing is due to biology, most of which we share with most other humans, and to environmental factors we share with countless others, we should find that some values are characteristic to particular cultures, and some to humanity more broadly.[12] There is most certainly a culture of analog. And where there is a shared culture, we should find shared values. Examining the values of analog means examining the meaningful activities of the participants in that culture. Let's start with a simple case.

Notes

1 Felix Richter, 'Despite Comeback, Vinyl Is Still Far From Its Glory Days', *Statista*, 19 April 2024, https://www.statista.com/chart/7699/lp-sales-in-the-united-states/ (accessed 7 March 2025); Patrick Leu, 'LP Album Unit Sales in the U.S. 1993-2023', *Statista*, 29 May 2024, https://www.statista.com/statistics/188822/lp-album-sales-in-the-united-states-since-2009/ (accessed 7 March 2025); Patrick Leu, 'Physical Album Shipments in the U.S. 1999-2023', *Statista*, 7 June

2024, https://www.statista.com/statistics/186772/album-shipments-in-the-us-music-industry-since-1999/ (accessed 7 March 2025).

2 Taylor Corporation (2025), 'The Vinyl Record Industry: Why Is There a Resurgence of Vinyl Records?', *Taylor.com*, August 5, https://www.taylor.com/blog/increased-vinyl-sales-and-the-vinyl-revival (accessed 12 September 2025); Christian Eede (2023), 'UK Vinyl Sales Increase for 16th Consecutive Year, With Over 5.9 million Sold in 2023', *DJ*, 20 December, https://djmag.com/news/uk-vinyl-sales-increase-16th-consecutive-year-over-59-million-sold-2023 (accessed 12 September 2025).

3 Statista, 'Board Games – Worldwide', *Statista*, January 2005, https://www.statista.com/outlook/cmo/toys-hobby/toys-games/board-games/worldwide (accessed 7 March 2025); D. Tighe, 'Board Games Market Value Worldwide from 2017 to 2023', *Statista*, 22 February 2024. https://www.statista.com/statistics/829285/global-board-games-market-value/ (accessed 7 March 2025).

4 Dimitrije Curcic, 'Independent Bookstores Statistics', *WordsRated*, 10 February 2023, https://wordsrated.com/independent-bookstores-statistics/ (accessed 7 March 2025).

5 Bill Rosenblatt, 'Luminate Data Music Report: The Album Is Once Again a Vinyl LP', *Forbes*, 24 May 2023, https://www.forbes.com/sites/billrosenblatt/2023/01/16/luminate-data-music-report-the-album-is-once-again-a-vinyl-lp/ (accessed 7 March 2025).

6 Jacques Ellul (1964), *The Technological Society*, trans. John Wilkinson (New York: Knopf), 20.

7 In Luigi Federico Menabrea (1843), 'Sketch of the Analytical Engine Invented by Charles Babbage, Esq', trans. with notes by Ada Lovelace, *Scientific Memoirs* 3: 666–731, at 710.

8 Jennifer Karns Alexander (2008), *The Mantra of Efficiency: From Waterwheel to Social Contract* (Baltimore: Johns Hopkins University Press), 2.

9 Alexander, *The Mantra of Efficiency*, 1.

10 John Dewey (1958), *Art as Experience* (New York: Capricorn Books), 27.

11 Anthony Weston (1987), 'Beyond Intrinsic Value: Pragmatism in Environmental Ethics', *Environmental Ethics* 7(4): 321–339, at 329.

12 See E.T. Mitchell (1945), 'Dewey's Theory of Valuation', *Ethics* 55(4): 287–297.

2

The Value of Material

Unboxing *Horrified: World of Monsters*

When I learn that board game publisher Ravensburger has released a fourth game in the *Horrified* series, I make a wide side-trip to Target on my way to work to pick up a copy. A lot of board games have expansions and variants, but the monster-themed *Horrified* is the only one I feel compelled to be a completist about. I don't tell Delaina I'm buying it. I leave the game in the car until the end of the day, when I can bring it home to open it up.

The box is smooth, with a satiny finish. It has a good heft—it's not a pillow, and it's not a brick. Rather than the usual shrink wrap, four clear round stickers hold the box closed. I can feel the gap between the box top and the bottom, and I run my fingertip along it. I work the edge of each sticker, at first with a thumbnail, then slowly pulling the sticker off to keep from damaging the box. Each sticker finally comes away from the cardboard with a satisfying *pop*. I rub away a little remaining glue residue with my fingers. I hold the box top by its edges and let the weight of the game pull the bottom out to land on the table: *sliiiip, plop*. Staring up from the open box is a giant eye—it's one illustrated quarter of the folded gameboard, which I lift off to set aside, but not without noticing the characteristic smell of the ink. Under the gameboard is an 8½ x 11″ instruction booklet, glossier than the box. I flip briefly through it, noticing the sound and texture of the paper as I do: *fwip, fwip, fwip*. Next is a resealable plastic bag containing cardstock mats. I work the bag's lips apart with my thumbs, then carefully get the plastic zip to open. I slide out the glossy cardstock mats, which catch on the zip corners a couple of times. Next are three thick 12 x 12″ cardboard sheets of tokens to be punched out, but they're shrink-wrapped together, and I set them aside for later. Finally, the interior of the box reveals itself. One large compartment holds another resealable baggie of colorful monster figurines, each about the size of my thumb. I don't open the baggie, but turn it about in my hand, examining the details and texture of the figurines. The bag is quite light. I set it aside and pick up the purple game bag beneath. The stitching around the bag is slipshod, but the bag has a nice plastic-canvas texture, and I tease apart the bag's Velcro tabs and open the bag like a little reuseable grocery bag. I put it back in the box, along with the baggie of figurines. In one of the smaller compartments are two more baggies—a tiny one with three garish six-sided dice, and a larger one with a dozen or so little plastic stands that slide around and *clinkle* like ice when I pick it up. I don't open these, but put both baggies back in their compartment (*clinkle-clinkle*), and retrieve a slim shrink-wrapped deck of cards from the final compartment. I start working to open the shrink wrap with a thumbnail, sticking small shreds to the circle stickers to keep them from blowing around, before I notice the tear-cord. I pull the tab, smoothly carving the cord around the deck and through the plastic, separating the top from the bottom. I rub my thumb over the glossy texture of the cards, lifting one a little from the deck before tapping it back, and putting the deck back in its compartment. I pick up the shrink-wrapped cardboard sheets I had earlier set aside. I work my thumbnail through the shrink wrap before tearing it away. It comes away easily, but static sticks it to my arm. Freeing myself from the shrink wrap, I start punching out tokens from the cardboard sheets. Each makes a *click-click-clack* as it comes out of its sheet and falls to the box lid below. This happens 116 times. *Click-click-clack, click-click, clack.*

I spent a lot of time and ink on that description of "unboxing" my new game because unboxing is something that board game enthusiasts *really* enjoy. And, frankly, who *doesn't* enjoy opening a present, even if it's a present from yourself? For those who haven't plunged into the hobby, the popularity of unboxing *videos* might be surprising. Growing increasingly popular as marketing tools for all manner of products, from toys to make-up, unboxing videos provide prospective customers with a better sense of what they are ordering over the Internet and help to build excitement for new products. Unboxing videos for *board games*, by contrast, are typically made by enthusiasts themselves rather than publishers.* These are usually entirely distinct from

---

*Publishers have nevertheless found ways to capitalize, sending free copies of their games to unboxers, who then film the unboxing.

the "how-to" videos made by publishers and reviewers to illustrate how the games actually *work* (increasingly useful in a hobby where instruction booklets often exceed 50 pages). Unboxing videos tap into something else. The best unboxing videos work to replicate the in-person unboxing experience, using sound to communicate the texture and heft of the materials and the experience of physically engaging with them. The best unboxing videos are *sumptuous*.[*] It probably doesn't go too far to suggest that unboxing videos are a kind of pornography—as "food porn" or "real estate porn" is a kind of pornography—serving as a substitute that tries to tap into our desire for the real, in-person experience. Philosophers C. Thi Nguyen and Bekka Williams offer an account of porn, broadly speaking,[†] suggesting that porn in all its forms offers a kind of immediate pleasure without the normal costs and complications of the real world (like spending $30 on a new game when you already own 50 you haven't played, or finding somewhere in the game room to put it).[1] But, like ordinary "porn-porn," unboxing videos can only go so far in approximating the real-world pleasures.

Opening a new game is a robust, multimodal experience, and the best game publishers design their packaging to *make* it an

---

[*]In this regard, there may be no better unboxing videos than those by Zunda Grapes (https://www.youtube.com/@ZUNDRAGRAPES). The fact that several of the games are in Russian is irrelevant since the videos contain no dialogue, focusing only on the material components of the games. Videos like these are sometimes described as "ASMR" unboxing videos, due to their ability to invoke a phenomenon called *autonomous sensory meridian response* in some viewers, a soothing or tingling sensation often associated with audio-visual stimuli.

[†]Nguyen and Williams are generalizing on an account of pornography originally offered by Michael Ray.

experience, layering components atop one other in deliberate order, nesting components in other components.* Today's board games often involve several elements that must be set up. Punched-out tokens in *Horrified: World of Monsters* must be separated by type. Most go in that little purple game bag, but others must be grouped together to be used with specific monsters in the game, set aside with their respective figurines and game mats. Some tokens are inserted into their plastic stands with an odd squishiness as the cardboard compresses. The board must be unfolded, the deck of cards separated into smaller decks, shuffled and stacked. Depending on the complexity of the game, it can be a rather involved process, and may require a rather large playing surface. Instruction booklets now normally include an image illustrating the ideal arrangement of elements. By contrast, there is really nothing to unpack or physically set up in a video game. Gamers learn the parts of the game by playing the game, normally skipping over all of that bothersome set-up to get right to it.† So, it might seem strange that board game publishers *lean into* the unboxing and set-up. But there is a value here.

The COVID-19 pandemic made us afraid to interact with things, to touch them, to breathe the air that others were breathing. And the digital realm promised an experience free of such terrors. Zoom meetings, streaming services, and video games promised all of the productivity, relaxation, and social

---

*Neil Patrick Harris's *Box ONE* contains packages with false bottoms and hidden pieces that only reveal themselves in gameplay.

†Some video games may include early set-up steps, like designing your characters, or laying out your armies, but these activities are really part of playing the game.

engagement without the risk. But what many of us learned in lockdown is that we *need* those sorts of interactions, and physical games, books, and music gave us at least some of what we needed.

By skipping over all of the set-up that comes with material board games, video game publishers were pursuing the value of efficiency highlighted by Jacques Ellul last chapter. In *Technology and the Character of Contemporary Life*, philosopher Albert Borgmann offers an alternative account, introducing what he calls "focal things and practices."[2] A focal practice, Borgmann suggests, is one that serves as a sort of center in our lives, engaging and invigorating us in a way that many of our daily and mundane activities do not.* Where efficient technology is meant to get us to our desired end as quickly and effortlessly as possible, minimizing our own labor and involvement, focal things and practices serve to engage us. "Focus," Borgmann notes, comes from the Latin word for "hearth"—the center of the home around which domestic life once revolved. The hearth provided light, nourishment, and heat for the home and the family:

> It assigned to the different family members tasks that defined their place in the household. The mother built the fire, the children kept the firebox filled, and the father cut the firewood. It provided for the entire family a regular and bodily engagement with the rhythm of the seasons that was woven

---

*My thanks to Ben Horne for pointing me at Borgmann's account. Tony Chackal's "Record Collecting as a Focal Practice" (2025) offers a much more thorough application of Borgmann's theory than I can do here.

together of the threat of cold and the solace of warmth, the smell of wood smoke, the exertion of sawing and of carrying, the teaching of skills, and the fidelity to daily tasks. These features of physical engagement and of family relations are only the first indication of the full dimensions of a thing's world. Physical engagement is not simply physical contact but the experience of the world through the sensibility of the body.[3]

A hearth required attention and patience, and brought the family together. As the domestic services offered by the hearth have gradually been taken on by self-cleaning ovens, central heating, and electric lights, and the hearth has shrunk to a fireplace lit perhaps only around the holidays, we have been left to seek the engagement and invigoration of the hearth in other things and practices.

Family game nights became something of a cultural touchpoint during the pandemic, drawing family members away from their screens and back to something like a hearth. The hearth is not valued primarily for its efficiency, but for its intimacy, immediacy, and warmth. A hearth isn't a box to be checked, a task to finish, but instead a place to gather, to linger. And what is a board game or jigsaw puzzle *for*, if not *gathering and lingering*?

Families and young couples stuck at home in lockdown quickly grew tired of the familiar games they grew up on—*Monopoly*, *Life*, *Risk*—and sought out new games. Many discovered *Settlers of Catan* and the world of "Eurogames," which tend to operate on a different philosophy than games in the American tradition. Will Arneson, author of *How to Host a Game Night*, says, "Every player is involved throughout the whole game. And even when it's other players' turns, you're not sitting around waiting. The games are always quite close. Nobody ever gets eliminated."[4] Rather than conflict-oriented games that depend heavily on luck and eliminate players from the table, Eurogames tend to rely on skill and resource collecting, keeping everybody at the table throughout the game, stoking the hearth.

Hearths aren't only to be found in the home, and lockdown made many of us keenly aware of those hearths outside the home that were no longer available to us. In his classic book, *The Great Good Place*, Ray Oldenburg introduced the notion of "third places"—vital places outside the home (the first place) or work (the second place) where people go to connect with their communities, to engage in "unplanned, unscheduled, unorganized, and unstructured" activities.[5] Oldenburg talks about coffee houses, pubs, and taverns, but we could as easily discuss board game cafés, which started spreading a few years before COVID, struggled more than most businesses to weather the pandemic, and are now exploding. A board game café is exactly what it sounds like—a coffee shop (or, increasingly, a taproom) with a board game library available to patrons. While I have been to board game cafés that charge players by the hour for the use of the table and the games (not unlike a pool hall), most that I have been to simply charge patrons one price to play as many games as they like, as long as they like, until closing time. Some don't charge anything at all for the use of their game libraries, assuming that the longer you stay,

the more food and drinks you will consume. Board game cafés are places to gather and linger.*

Some games simply can't be played in a virtual space, or over Zoom. Card games like *Anomia*, *Stroop*, and *Rock!* are all about the frenetic slapping down of cards. "Dexterity" games like *Jenga*, *Suspend*, and *Catch the Moon* involve the careful and delicate placement of game pieces, where shaky hands or misjudged weight might mean disaster. Other games, like *Crokinole*, *PitchCar*, and *Catacombs* are all about flicking wooden disks—at central targets, around a track, or at each other's wooden disks.

*As are record stores, comic stores, used book stores, and other places where analog objects are bought, sold, and traded. See Brandon Polite and Aaron Meskin's "Why Record Shops Matter Aesthetically" (2025).

Some games are simply *better* in-person. Despite the enormous popularity of online poker, which is fast-paced (efficient) and lets you play at home in your underwear (convenient), many prefer to seek out in-person games, sometimes traveling long distances to do so.* Psychologist Maria Konnikova, who took a deep dive into poker in her bestseller *The Biggest Bluff*, observes that "somehow, online doesn't feel like real life even though the money is real enough."[6] *Washington Post* columnist Norman Chad, who resorted to online poker during lockdown, writes, "It feels lonely and sterile."[7] Even when a game doesn't *demand* in-person interaction, the sterility of online approximations leaves out the richness of shared in-person experience: the smell of coffee brewing in the next room, the rattle of the table whenever someone leans their elbows on it, the muscle fatigue and frustration of attempting to hold a massive hand of *UNO* cards. Delaina points out how much I *hate* it when people rattle the table with their elbows—and everybody hates muscle fatigue—but that *richness* of experience isn't replicable in a digital environment, and I'll trade off some annoyance for that rich experience.

Let's talk about the importance of *touch*.

---

*Whether online or in-person, poker is about making decisions with incomplete information. Online poker is about constantly calculating the sea of shifting odds based on what cards you can see. In-person poker is messier; it's about reading people. A 2013 study by Michael Slepian showed that while watching a poker player's overall body language gave a casual observer no better than chance at determining a bluff, and observing the player's face in particular actually dropped prediction *below* chance, observing a player's *hands* noticeably increased performance. See Slepian, Young, Rutchick, and Ambady "Quality of Professional Players' Poker," and Chapter 11 of Maria Konnikova's *The Biggest Bluff* (2020).

Touching Art

Children need to touch, exploring the world with their hands, their mouths. Jean Piaget's famous model of cognitive development highlights the importance of touch at the earliest stage, the sensorimotor, lasting from birth through the first two years of childhood. Touch is the primary way that young children engage with and learn about the world. But, as childhood gives way to adolescence and then to adulthood, development is expected to move from the concrete to the abstract, the sensuous to the intellectual. "Look with your eyes," my mother told me more than once, "not with your hands." Everything you need to know, it was suggested to me, can be learned from a distance. Increasingly, our physical interactions with the world are concentrated in our fingertips as we type on keyboards and swipe on touchscreens. But that urge to engage with the world through touch never entirely goes away, does it?

When you see a hulking Henry Moore bronze or the bright sea of fabric making up a Katharina Grosse installation, don't you *want* to touch it? When you see a Van Gogh on the gallery wall, with its thick brushstrokes like frozen waves of pigment, don't you *want* to run your fingers along them? You're not alone. Art critic Hettie Judah writes:

> I am every conservator's nightmare – that person who wants to touch the art. I long to glide my palm over curving marble, test the weight of small bronzes and fall into the soft embrace of tangled fibre. In a quiet gallery, unwatched, I once nestled my face into the tufted wool of a Sheila Hicks wall hanging and inhaled its maternal lanolin.[8]

A security guard at the British Museum reports, "You stop a hundred people touching and there are 200 more . . . It's like trying to turn back the sea."[9]

Art historian and literary critic Herbert Read suggests that sculpture in particular is an artform *meant* to be felt as much as it is to be seen. Modern sculpture especially, he argues, should be understood as "a three-dimensional mass occupying space and only to be apprehended by senses that are alive to its volume and ponderability, as well as to its visual appearance."[10] Read calls sculpture the "art of *palpation*—an art that gives satisfaction in the touching and handling of objects."[11] Read's claim gave rise to a famous feud with fellow modern art critic Clement Greenberg, who argued that primary and proper engagement with sculpture is optical.[12] I would press Read's view further, in fact, and propose that *all* of the museum's holdings, from the cold bronze sculptures to the linen paper, promise tactile satisfaction. Museologist Fiona Candlin suggests that one central reason that museum visitors want to touch the displays is because we want to *learn* more about what we're merely seeing, and we *can't* learn everything with our eyes.[13] Sometimes we need to learn it with our hands or (if we're like Hettie Judah) our faces. And when we can't, we know we're missing something.

Now, the reasons you're not allowed to touch most of the displays in the gallery are usually pretty clear, though every so often we get a reminder. In August 2024, at a visit to the Hecht Museum in Haifa, Israel, a four-year-old boy wandered away from his father and pulled over a 3,500-year-old jar that was displayed without protective glass.[14] The jar shattered when it hit the ground. The museum, however, defended its choice to display archaeological artifacts in a manner that puts them at such risk. "Whenever possible, items are displayed without barriers or glass walls," the Museum said in a statement. "The museum believes that there is a special charm in experiencing an archaeological find without any obstructions."[15] This is part of a new trend in museums.

Museums and galleries have long worked to separate collections from visitors in all but the visual and auditory modes. This coincides with a longstanding philosophical prioritization of sight and sound over touch, taste, and smell, a prejudice that goes back at least as far as ancient Greece.[16] Aristotle argued that the visual and the auditory are essentially cognitive and intellectual, while the pleasures derived from touch, taste, and smell were essentially animalistic.[17] Following Aristotle,

Renaissance philosopher and Catholic priest Marsilio Ficino suggested that taste, smell, and touch could only sense what is nearby, and so are essentially material, while hearing and sound can sense what is remote, and so are more closely associated with the soul—something that animals notoriously lack.[18] By the late eighteenth century, just as the notion of Fine Art was emerging in Western Europe and public art museums were being conceived, Immanuel Kant was arguing that aesthetic appreciation was an essentially intellectual affair, providing exercise for the mental faculties as perhaps gymnasiums provided exercise for bodies.* Kant famously describes the enjoyment of beauty as arising from "free play of the imagination."[19] In his *Lectures on Anthropology*, Kant calls hearing a "play of sensation" and sight a "play of shape."[20] And unlike the other senses, Kant suggests, they are shareable: "The more humans can share in them, the nobler are the senses, and the more they make objects mutual for us. And these are also the most social."[21] Sight and hearing allow for mutual enjoyment, where taste and smell are subjective, chemical, and personal. "Feeling," Kant says, "does not participate at all" in shared enjoyment.[22] So, where the Fine Arts have come to be associated with the "higher" senses of sight and sound, and put in museums and galleries, the "lower" senses have been left to perfumes, to food and drink, and to clothing—things of ordinary life, unworthy of serious aesthetic concern.

*The Louvre opened in 1793. Kant published his *Critique of Judgment*—his third critique, focused on aesthetics—in 1790.

But things are changing. More and more museums want to put visitors in literal touch with their collections, or at least to provide a suitable simulation. Ezgi Ucar, an intern at New York's Metropolitan Museum of Art, knows what it's like:

> I think everyone has had the urge to touch, smell, or taste at least one of the Museum's objects. I was immediately fascinated by the beautiful figures in the Arts of Africa, Oceania, and the Americas galleries, and I found myself particularly interested in the Power Figure (*Nkisi N'Kondi: Mangaaka*). I wanted to touch and smell it mainly because of the variety of materials it includes (wood, metal, resin, and shell) and the materials that were added to the figure during rituals, like dirt from burial sites; white clay from riverbeds; and nails, blades, and other hardware.
>
> I decided to create a small, touch-sensitive replica of the figure that would have its own smell and sound. I used clay and nails similar to the materials used to make the sculpture. I then put a little bit of essential oil on the top of the sculpture to simulate the original scent of the object.[23]

Ucar's creations are part of the Met's Media Lab, where the Museum's staff work to find new ways for visitors to engage with their collections. Museums seem to understand the yearning that visitors feel to move beyond the visual and the auditory.*

*In 2005, Hugh Aldersey-Williams and Lauren Parker curated the "Touch Me" exhibition at the Victoria and Albert Museum in London on the idea that, in the modern computer age, our day-to-day interactions offer only "impoverished tactual experiences" (Candlin, *Art, Museums and Touch*, 160).

And while the extraordinarily valuable items will remain behind velvet ropes and (in the case of the *Mona Lisa*) bulletproof glass, museums seem to be trying to give visitors just enough of the tactile experience of art objects to scratch that itch. We value physical interactions because we are, after all, physical beings. Why should we expect to find complete fulfillment in the purely intellectual realm? Psychologist Tiffany Field notes, "Touch, affecting both tactile and pressure receptors, stimulates the central nervous system into a state of relaxation. Anxiety and stress levels, both behavioral and biochemical, are then reduced and the general effect is a more relaxed, more attentive state."[24]

Make It Real

In 1991, artist Nick Bantock published two books. The first was a pop-up book adaptation of Lewis Carroll's poem, *Jabberwocky*.* The second was *Griffin and Sabine*, which might best be described as a sort of literary pop-up novel. More specifically, *Griffin and Sabine* is an epistolary novel, told in postcards and letters exchanged by the book's title characters. The postcards are beautifully illustrated, with one side of the postcard on one side of the page, and the other on the other, the writing often referring to the image, prompting the reader to flip the page back and forth several times. The letters, meanwhile, are on loose paper, folded and tucked into envelopes affixed to the page, which must

*It was Bantock's third pop-up, following *There Was an Old Lady* and *Wings*.

be opened, unfolded, read, and returned before the reader can continue the story. The book had an original print run of 10,000 copies, but that wasn't nearly enough. *Griffin and Sabine* became a series, the first three books spending more than 100 weeks on the *New York Times* bestseller list.[25]

Librarian Brenda Ross writes in *Info Cafe*, the blog for the Davenport, Iowa, Public Library:

> It seems like it would be a nightmare for public libraries to keep track of the loose pieces, and part of me is reluctant to tell anyone else about them for fear of tempting fate . . . but I feel it wouldn't be fair to keep something so enjoyable under wraps. I am grateful and pleased to report to you that not once in my history of repeatedly checking out these books from multiple libraries do I recall ever encountering a missing or ill-treated piece. This is a great credit to Bantock's readers and I would like to take this opportunity to thank each and every one of them for taking such good care of these treasures![26]

Bantock's books are all *participatory* in a way that brings the reader's attention to their materiality, and demands a careful sort of hands-on engagement with the objects. When Bantock tried years later to gather support for a series of interactive apps for digital devices based on the *Griffin and Sabine* series, the project did not meet its crowdsourcing goal.[27] To me, this is no great surprise: how could my iPhone hope to give me any of what a print copy of the *Griffin and Sabine* gives me? Who wants a digital pop-up book?

Material is inevitably, irreducibly multimodal. Watch people in a bookstore, particularly a used bookstore. They visibly sniff the air when they enter the store.* They run their fingers along the spines on a shelf. They pick books off the shelf, trace their fingers across embossed covers, flip the pages without reading them. In the material realm, something *without* a smell, or *without* a texture, is still notable for what it lacks. The digital, by contrast, is by its nature audiovisual, and we tend not to notice what it's missing until we have something to compare it to.

In a review, James Austin of the *New York Times* notes of the tile-laying game *Azul*: "the Bakelite pieces are satisfyingly clicky."[28] "Satisfying" is a word that gets used a lot by board game enthusiasts to describe their interactions with game pieces. There *are* several online apps offering virtual board game experiences, and they are popular. *Tabletop Simulator* on the Steam platform lets users set up digital versions of analog games, some with surprisingly good digital recreations of play, including flipping cards, rolling dice, and so on.† *Tabletop Simulator* skips over all of that set-up we were talking about earlier. "Not all games suit the virtual world," however, says game reviewer Jon Purkis. "Anything with lots of fiddly bits is a nightmare."[29] For many gamers,

---

*The smell of a used bookstore is usually the smell of the acid in cheap paperbacks breaking down the paper; it is the smell of the paper eating itself. Different paper compositions will give that smell a hint of vanilla or almond or coffee or must. In a 2014 (now-deleted) tweet, literary scholar Oliver Tearle coined the word "bibliosmia" to describe the act of smelling books.

†Most of these are user-created "mods," with home-scanned elements, and are of varying quality. They are also usually created without the permission of the copyright owners.

though, the fiddly bits are a good part of the value of playing. Fiddly bits require active attention and physical interaction, heightening immersion in the game.* For some, the efficiency of playing online, especially when you can't get together with friends, and especially when it overcomes the cost of paying for an authorized copy of the game, may outweigh the value of analog play. But it is most certainly a tradeoff. A digital version of *Azul* could replicate the tile-placement mechanic, and could even accompany it with an appropriate "clicky" sound, but the satisfaction that Austin talks about comes from the sound *as it arises from physically interacting with the pieces. Tabletop Simulator* lacks the *haptic* link between the player and the tiles.†

"Haptic" describes the array of sensory information related to touch, bodily position, and bodily movement. Since the 1970s, game engineers have experimented with haptic technology, starting with Sega's *Fonz*, a motorcycle racing game that combined a digital display with "authentic" sounds and replica motorcycle handlebars to control gameplay: "Turn the handlebars, and you

---

*In his *Aesthetics of Virtual Reality* (2021), philosopher Grant Tavinor is rankled by loose use of the term "immersion" in the field of VR studies, calling it ambiguous, opaque, and contradictory (119). Little rankles analytic philosophers more than ordinary use of language. Tavinor defines immersion as "the sense of being taken up completely with an activity and forgetting the world beyond that activity" (115). Illustrating my own analytic tendencies, I would suggest that "completely" and "forgetting" are a tad strong. For a definition of "immersion," I would prefer something closer to "absorbing involvement" (the Merriam-Webster definition), which I think tracks ordinary usage.

†Virtual jigsaw puzzles exist, too, and they are exactly what you think they are. Point, click, drag, and (in fancier versions) rotate pieces to build an image. Putting together a virtual jigsaw is oddly reminiscent of playing *Minesweeper*.

corner and bank with startling realism. Twist the handle throttle open, and you accelerate along with the rising scream of your high compression engine. Collide with another bike—the handlebars vibrate and the TV screen flashes a reverse image."[30] "Startling realism" might be a bit strong, but that haptic ingredient proved to be a critical link to the *real.* As video games moved from public arcades to home game systems, game controllers developed several varieties of haptic feedback mechanism in an attempt to maximize immersion.* More than sight, more than sound, the sense of touch gives a sense of *presence*, something virtual reality researchers treat as key to creating perceived reality in immersive virtual environments.[31] Physical interaction with the world comes with its own immediate feedback: we push and the world pushes back.†

Carolyn Korsmeyer notes that, as far back as Aristotle, philosophers have treated the sense of touch as what most reliably grounds us in a sense of reality. This, despite the long

*Michael Schiess, Founder of the Pacific Pinball Museum, speaks to the perhaps-surprising endurance of pinball machines: "The video arcade died out because the games were better on your home computer. But people are longing for interactivity, amongst themselves in a social environment, and they also like the tactile feeling of pinball" (Wired, "How Pinball Survived Video Games, the Mob and Politics"). Since the late 1970s, pinball machines have actually been hybrid digital/analog machines. The scorekeeping mechanisms of early machines simply couldn't keep up with the speed of the players. Today, pinball gameplay is mechanical—analog—but scoring and pixelated displays are digital. Game designers use the digital elements for their efficiency, but retain the analog because it gives us something the digital struggles to replicate: an immersive, multimodal experience.

†That's just Newton's third law.

tradition of separating the material from the intellectual. The mind, after all, has a way of playing tricks, and uncertainty about what the other senses are telling us can usually be quickly resolved with a simple touch. Visual and auditory illusions are common, and taste and smell are radically subjective, but touch seems anchored to reality. And, when other sense data are connected to touch—as with the clicky tiles of *Azul*—it grounds those in reality, too.*

A lot of analog enthusiasts talk about analog as being "real." David Sax writes,

> Why a book? Why print? Because it is real. Because I can hold this very book in my hands once it is printed, see my name on the cover, and know that all the work was worth it, regardless of how many copies it sells. That feeling is the ultimate luxury, and it is one I will happily pay for, time and again, as a reader and a writer.[32]

My friend Laura recently published her second book, her first novel. Because Amazon operates as a sort of funnel, filling

---

*Psychologists studying multimodal phenomena—where an experience folds in some combination of visual, tactile, auditory, and other sense phenomena—note that responses to multimodal stimuli are typically greater than the combined response to each of the discrete sense data. "In other words," writes psychologist Lorin Lacks, "if you presented the stimulus in one modality at a time and measured the response to each of these unimodal stimuli, you would find that adding them together would still not equal the response to the multimodal stimulus" (Lachs, "Multi-Modal Perception"). A fully multimodal experience, where sensory input is appropriately linked together and not merely additive, is greater than the sum of its parts.

and emptying its warehouses as quickly as possible, and has the girth to ignore the wishes of small university presses, it sent out preordered copies to buyers a month before the book's official release, and I got my copy in the mail before Laura had received her own from the publisher. She had seen the page proofs of the book any number of times, but she was ecstatic to be handed a physical copy of the book when my wife and I walked it over to her house, just down the street. To Laura, *that object matters*. Another friend of mine, Casey, an artist, regularly sells prints of his works to those who can't afford the hefty price tags on the original paintings. "Please sign it," he is asked: "Please add a little sketch or doodle to the print"—a *remarque*. Please make it *individual*, make it *real*.

Aura and the Individual

Physical objects have physical history. Consider J.J. Abrams and Doug Dorst's *S*, a sort of metanovel published by Mulholland Books. Although the project saw print in 2013, the genesis of the book started years earlier when Abrams found a worn Robert Ludlum paperback, seemingly discarded, at the Los Angeles airport. In the book was a note, telling whoever found it to read it and then leave it somewhere else for someone else to find it.* Abrams says that he was reminded of his days at Sarah Lawrence College, studying from books marked up with others' marginal notes and highlighting. After several years, Abrams teamed up with author Doug Dorst to realize an idea he had been mulling.[33] At the core of *S* is another novel written by Dorst—V.M. Straka's *Ship of Theseus*, a self-standing and layered story about conspiracy theories and assassination plots. The copy in the reader's hands purports to be a copy from the collection of the Laguna Verde High School Library. Library stamps in the front and back cover and a library sticker with the book's Dewey Decimal location affixed to the spine attest to the object's apparent history. In the book's margins are handwritten notes by two readers, Eric and Jen, who use the book to communicate about Straka and their own lives. Like Bantock's *Griffin and Sabine*, *S* requires an

*Abrams may be describing a book participating in the Bookcrossing book club. Participants affix a sticker to a book, telling whoever finds it to take it, read it, check in at BookCrossing.com, and "release" the book again in a public place for someone else to find it. The project was launched in 2001 and continues today.

involved sort of experience on the reader's part. Flipping through the pages, the reader will discover handwritten letters, a postcard, a mimeographed telegram, and more tucked in the pages, offering clues to the metastory and driving the further narrative. The pages of the book are yellowed. The spine of the book is worn. It *feels* like the object it purports to be.* And it reminds the reader that the book is, after all, an *object*. The copy of *Oedipus Rex* that you purchased used at the campus bookstore was someone *else's* book before it was yours. There are traces of that person in it. Highlights, underlines, marginal notes. It is not merely *a* copy of *Oedipus Rex*; it is *that* copy of *Oedipus Rex*.

The object has what art historian Alois Riegl called "age value."[34] While historical value is simply the importance of some art object in a chain of events, Riegl writes, age value is that which reveals itself in the imperfections that accumulate in an object with age and decay. Old things, Riegl says, should *look* old, and it's that "natural" aging that Dorst and Abrams are working to simulate in *S.*† Philosopher Yuriko Saito writes:

> Aged objects such as old relics, ruins, musty books, and tattered and frayed objects exemplify the effects of the march of time, without succumbing completely to its dictate. If they wholly disintegrate, they are no longer fit for positive aesthetic

---

*Alas, it doesn't smell like that object. Readers of a certain age will remember mimeographs, and will probably (like me) lift up the telegram to sniff it. They will sadly be disappointed, the illusion briefly shattered.

†Riegl says that "Signs of decay (premature aging) in new works disturb us just as much as signs of new production (conspicuous restorations) in old works" (Riegl, "The Modern Cult of Monuments", 73). As such, *S should* be disturbing to the reader, but then so should deliberately distressed furniture and jeans.

appreciation. Those objects we do appreciate are the ones which are in the process of decay, before losing their identity and integrity altogether. What they present to us can be characterized variously as tension, balance, dialogue, or dialectic relationship between two opposing forces: nature's own process and our attempt (via what we create) at defying and counteracting it.[35]

Brandon Polite and Elizabeth Scarbrough focus on the particular age value of vinyl records:*

> The pops and clicks a record acquires over time are technically defects caused by damage; yet, along with the crackle of static from the stylus moving along the grooves, they can add richness to the experience of listening to an old record. . . . Where digital formats offered clarity and precision, they also removed the traces of wear and time that many listeners came to associate with genuineness and individuality. Vinyl's sonic patina, once dismissed as a mere limitation of the format, was reimagined as a feature rather than a flaw.[36]

Cycling enthusiasts talk about "beausage," a portmanteau of "beauty" and "usage," coined by Grant Petersen in his 2012 book, *Just Ride*:

---

*After the manuscript for this book was written, but before it went to the printers, Polite and Scarbrough's essay, "Patina of Sound" (2025), appeared in *Espes*. I knew they were working on an essay on vinyl as it intersects with Carolyn Korsmeyer's work, but hadn't read it. I was delighted to see that their essay intersects with this chapter (and the next) at several points. Clearly, I'm not the only one who recognizes the values of analog.

> In 1992 or so, at the Interbike trade show in Las Vegas, there was a 1952 Bianchi that had been ridden by Fausto Coppi, a famous racer from the '40s and '50s. The bar tape was tattered, 20 percent of the paint was worn away, and the leather saddle was well worn and looked like it had been ridden by a guy who didn't want a new saddle because he hadn't completely worn out the old one. It was the best-looking bike at the show, and the only one with beausage.[37]

Essentially, beausage is the beauty that a thing gains through use rather than mere natural decay, and without rendering the object dysfunctional. More than that, it is beauty *associated with* use—the beauty of a thing that has seen some mileage, and looks like it has some more in it.

Both age value and beausage are qualities had by particular objects—individual material things. The used copy of *Oedipus Rex* that you bought at the campus bookstore shows its age and its use in the yellowing of its paper, the dogearing of its corners, the dings on its edges, and the highlights and scribblings that mark its pages. The play written by Sophocles has none of these things, though it certainly has historical value. And a copy made from *my* copy might *document* my copy's age, but it doesn't *replicate* it. Theorist Walter Benjamin famously had something to say about this:

> Even the most perfect reproduction of a work of art is lacking in one element: its presence in time and space, its unique existence at the place where it happens to be. This unique existence of the work of art determined the history to which

> it was subject throughout the time of its existence. This includes the changes which it may have suffered in physical condition over the years as well as the various changes in its ownership.[38]

What the reproduction lacks, Benjamin calls "aura."

Aura has always been treated as a funny thing in philosophy, ever since Benjamin introduced it into discourse. And it comes up a *lot*. That is, it gets *mentioned* a lot by philosophers of art, but usually in passing, not in print. The problem seems to be that theorists are never quite sure how to treat it, though it appears to strike at something intuitive that many latch onto. For his part, Benjamin doesn't seem overly interested in clarifying the notion, which has a way of mutating through his writings.* In broad strokes, we might think of aura as being close to that "special charm" that the Hecht Museum was talking about—that only comes across in the immediate presence of the genuine article. Benjamin attached the notion of aura to the quality of *authenticity*, which he says only the original has, which it carries with it through time and place. Whether Benjamin thinks of aura as a property of the object or as a quality of the *experience*

---

*Benjamin often talks like the Sphinx. Cultural theorist Miriam Bratu Hansen notes, "Anything but a clearly delimited, stable concept, aura describes a cluster of meanings and relations that appear in Benjamin's writings in various configurations and not always under its own name; it is this conceptual fluidity that allows aura to become such a productive nodal point in Benjamin's thinking" (Hansen, "Benjamin's Aura," 339). It's also what annoys analytic philosophers. More often than not, thinkers are inclined to introduce their *own* notions of aura rather than attempt to analyze Benjamin's (see, e.g., Thomas Leddy's *The Extraordinary in the Ordinary* and Michael Betancourt's *The Critique of Digital Capitalism*).

of the object is unclear.* Perhaps it doesn't matter. What *does* matter, at least to Benjamin, is that aura is *withering* "in the age of mechanical reproduction."[39] This isn't an altogether odd notion. Think about your favorite Taylor Swift album. A studio album does not capture live performance, but consists in cobbled-together pieces of multiple performance "takes" and studio-layered sounds that are mixed in a surprisingly complicated and technical way—surprising even if you have a basic grasp of what's involved: Taylor Swift's 2020 song "Willow" is made up of nearly 100 tracks mixed together.† In most cases today, all of this is done digitally.‡ In the end, a digital "master" is produced, and this master can be perfectly reproduced, over and over again, without any loss to the file or the sound. The digital master is typically stored on a hard drive or magnetic tape. But, while any given digital storage device containing a copy of the digital master may be designated *the master*, these must be periodically copied to *new* digital masters as digital storage materials tend to corrode over time, and changes in technology require migrating digital files periodically to new formats. In a very real sense, there *is* no original, there probably never was. Philosophers talk in terms of *types* and *tokens*. The "type" is the *work*—say, Swift's "Willow." It exists as a *track* exemplified by the digital master.[40]

---

*Related to the notion that aura is a property of an object that cannot be copied with its other properties, Medieval philosophers introduced the notion of a *haecceity*—a self-identifying property. I might perfectly copy what a thing looks like, its size, color, shape, and mass, but I cannot copy the property that makes it the thing that it is. Haecceities are not reproducible.

†For a very deep dive, see Tingen, "Taylor Swift 'willow.'"

‡"Willow" was mixed with Pro Tools, the industry standard.

But any other accurate copy of that track is as much an authentic example of "Willow" as any other—each is a "token of the type." Similar stories can be told for your favorite film and your favorite novel. In mass media, in ordinary cases, there is simply no original to have aura.*

Benjamin, writing in 1935, thinks of this as a shattering of tradition. *Traditionally*, artworks were copied manually—repainted by students, performed by musicians and actors, copied and recopied by hand. And each copy that came about through this sort of practice had its own aura. Going back to the earliest cave paintings and carved fertility statues, art objects had their value in what Benjamin calls "cult value." As long as Scriptures needed to be copied by hand and songs sung in person, they continued to embody a ritual value. But the printing press, the photograph, and the phonograph took art reproduction out of art traditions and out of sacred rituals and distributed art to the masses. Technology industrialized art, and ritual values were replaced with exhibition value. Art objects became ordinary things, and authenticity ceased to be a concern.

---

*Walter Benjamin first published his essay in 1935, when all of this was still analog. Albums were recorded and edited on *tape*, filmmakers shot on *film*, and writers used *ink*. Some still do. Musician Jack White strictly records on analog tape, Quentin Tarantino films exclusively on analog film, and Danielle Steel has apparently written all of her nearly 200 books on a 1946 Olympia typewriter (Tingen, "Inside Track: Jack White"; Leathan, "Quentin Tarantino Explains Why He Shoots on Film"; Beard, "Life's Work"). Still, Jack White's Third Man Records releases all of their albums both on vinyl and digitally, digital movie projectors have been the industry standard for a quarter century (and there is no analog streaming service), and somebody at Penguin Random House has to scan all of Danielle Steel's manuscripts before they can be turned into files that the printer can work with.

In analog culture, we find an embrace of ritual and a return to Borgmann's *hearth*. We build new traditions. When Delaina and I sit down to work on a jigsaw puzzle that has been passed on to us from a friend, we pick an album from the collection, slide the vinyl record from its case, give it a quick dust, and put it on the turntable. Lowering the needle, a little light crackling comes through the speakers before the needle finds its groove and the music starts playing. Most of our records have been thrifted from Goodwill and garage sales. Many have cases that are held together with packing tape. Several survived a flood in our last house. A few have undergone surgery as Delaina has taken them to the lab to correct skips with a carefully-handled needle under a microscope. So, when we listen to that record, we are not merely listening to *a* copy of *Persuasive Percussion III* or *Meaty, Beaty, Big and Bouncy*; we are listening to *our* copy of *Persuasive Percussion III*, *our* copy of *Meaty, Beaty, Big and Bouncy*.* I know where we got each of these albums; I know what they have been through since. And when we finish that jigsaw puzzle, we will sign the back of the last piece we put into place, as our friends did before us, and we will pass *that* puzzle on to other friends, signatures and all. These are tokens of types, but they are also *individuals* with individual histories and age value.† This is how I

*Most of the music I listened to as a kid was on the 8-track cassettes that I claimed, and that my father had long since put aside. To this day, streaming Meat Loaf's *Bat Out of Hell* while I do the dishes, I know where the characteristic *ca-chunk* of the 8-track switching tracks would occur in the middle of a song.

†My copy of *Horrified: World of Monsters* is a token of the type, no different in design from any other copy on Target's shelf. But it is also an individual, and age value is a quality of individuals. The longer I own it, the more age value that individual will develop.

experience them. My engagement with the material token is the experience of an individual thing, and not merely a type. I can't touch a type.*

Benjamin announced the withering of aura in the age of mechanical reproduction, but the embrace of analog—in family game nights and game cafés, in jigsaw puzzling sessions while listening to vinyl records, in passing along a dogeared Ludlum paperback to a stranger at an airport—revitalizes it again. Old traditions of the hearth return and new traditions arise. The analog embraces the individual. This is a return of aura.†

Return to the Hearth

Albert Borgmann writes, "In the technological setting, the culture of the table not only focuses our life; it is also distinguished as a place of healing, one that restores us to the depth of the world and to the wholeness of our being."[41] Engagement with analog, by its nature, demands more attention, offering a fuller, richer, more multimodal experience. When it is my turn in

*Delaina and I have collections of records, of puzzles, of board games, of books and comics. A collection of this sort is not a set in the abstract sense—a *set* is just a meaningless assemblage of things. A collection is an assemblage of *individuals*. One game we own, *Discover: Lands Unknown*, embraces this notion by selling each copy of the game with a random selection of modular board pieces and game cards. So, I and my friend up the street might both own *Discover: Lands Unknown*, but we own distinct individuals. And as obvious as this is for *Discover: Lands Unknown*, it is also true for our respective copies of any other game, book, or album.

†I owe this observation to Sam Martin.

Horrified, I must attend to cards, meeples, and other game pieces. The presence of others at the table (even—or especially—when their elbows wobble the table) keeps me present as well. When the needle reaches the end of the album, I have to get up and flip the record if I want to hear more music. The turntable must be attended to; it won't simply start playing another album on its own. If I start nodding off reading my book, it will fall to the floor, I will lose my page, and I will have to find it again.

Vinyl enthusiasts often argue for the richer quality of sound that a vinyl record offers, when compared to what's found on an MP3 or other digital option. In truth, I can't usually tell the difference between them—and unless you have an extremely high-end stereo system, you probably can't either.* But I *do* tend

---

*A vinyl record produces sound when a needle works its way through the record's spiraling groove. On each side of that groove are microscopic waves of vinyl that vibrate the needle. The turntable converts these vibrations into an electrical signal that it sends through an amplifier to the speakers, which use magnets to vibrate the speaker's diaphragm, producing sound. When I stream music from my iPod, it arrives on my device as packets of zeros and ones, which the streaming software converts into electrical signals, which it sends to the same speakers. In order to speed up the streaming or download process of a digital file, that data is often compressed by removing frequencies that fall outside the typical range of human hearing and squeezing higher frequencies into lower ranges. Essentially, compression tends to move sounds toward the mid-range. The more the file is compressed—typically—the muddier the sound. Some file formats are "lossier" than others, eliminating detail and clarity. Some are touted as "lossless." High-end speakers divide frequencies into different "drivers" (like woofers and tweeters) to clarify sounds and use higher-end materials that won't distort the sound, producing a higher signal-to-noise ratio (SNR). Higher-end speakers operate at a wider range of frequences than lower-end speakers and have less distortion and noise. If we're dealing with a vinyl copy and a digital stream, both ultimately from the same master, the vinyl copy risks the pops and clicks that tend to come with age, and the digital copy risks muddying through compression. But much of that difference won't be detectable on most people's home

to have a richer *experience* of the music, because I'm actually *listening* to it. I engage with my vinyl records in a way that I don't tend to engage with music that I've just set up my iPad to stream, and so I tend to attend to it more. Listening to vinyl is, by its nature, a more *intentional* experience, and so I will tend to listen more closely and more deeply than I might to whatever is streaming over Spotify. Benjamin notes, "A man who concentrates before a work of art is absorbed by it. He enters into this work of art the way legend tells of the Chinese painter when he viewed his finished painting. In contrast, the distracted mass absorbs the work of art."[42] In one ear, out the other.

The nature of analog media—including their general inconvenience and inefficiency—requires our attention more than do their digital equivalents, and our attention is rewarded. In handling material, our attention is enhanced. We take in details that we ignore—or which are hidden from or unavailable to us—in digital environments. Streamed music tends to drift to the background, as the mind easily drifts from Zoom meetings and online reading. But the hearth is warm and tends to be experienced more deeply. Though we linger at the hearth, the richness of experience that it offers and the attention that it demands tend to keep us in the here and now. Analog has a way of anchoring us, and of calling to us from our screens.

---

audio speakers. And, if we have brand new vinyl and lossless digital, they should sound essentially the same. As Zed Adams ("Surface Noise") points out, "tape hiss" audible in playing analog magnetic tape recordings is another issue, though this too can be reduced with quality of tape and noise-reduction systems like Dolby NR and DBX.

Notes

1 Michael C. Rea (2001), 'What Is Pornography?' *Noûs* 35(1): 118–145; C. Thi Nguyen and Bekka Williams (2020), 'Moral Outrage Porn', *Journal of Ethics and Social Philosophy* 18(2): 147–172. For a more accessible introduction to the theory, see C. Thi Nguyen and Bekka Williams, 'Why We Call Things "Porn"', *New York Times*, 26 July 2019, https://www.nytimes.com/2019/07/26/opinion/sunday/porn.html (accessed 7 March 2025). Sarah Worth provides an excellent study of food porn in Chapter 5 of her 2021 book, *Taste: A Philosophy of Food* (London: Reaktion Books).

2 Albert Borgmann (1984), *Technology and the Character of Contemporary Life: A Philosophical Inquiry* (Chicago: University of Chicago Press), 4.

3 Ibid., 41–42.

4 Rob Schmitz, 'Sales Of "Settlers Of Catan" Skyrocket During Coronavirus Crisis', *NPR*, 4 August 2020, https://www.npr.org/2020/08/04/898853332/sales-of-settlers-of-catan-skyrocket-during-coronavirus-crisis (accessed 7 March 2025).

5 Ray Oldenburg (1999), *The Great Good Place* (New York: Marlowe & Company), 31.

6 Maria Konnikova (2020), *The Biggest Bluff* (New York: Penguin), 51.

7 Norman Chad, 'Being forced to play poker online serves as another reminder of why we need human contact', *Washington Post*, 19 April 2020, https://www.washingtonpost.com/sports/being-forced-to-play-poker-online-serves-as-another-reminder-of-why-we-need-human-contact/2020/04/19/fb624a2c-8258-11ea-a3eb-e9fc93160703_story.html (accessed 7 March 2025).

8 Hettie Judah (2024), '"Painting is a bodily activity": Hettie Judah on the more sensory pleasures of art', *Apollo* 199(730): 33–34, at 33.

9 Marlen Komar (2019), 'Why touching art is so tempting – and exciting', *CNN*, 13 May 2019, https://www.cnn.com/style/article/why-we-want-to-touch-art/index.html (accessed 7 March 2025).

10 Herbert Read (1956), *The Art of Sculpture* (New York: Pantheon Books), ix.

11 Ibid., 49.

12 See David J. Getsy (2011), 'Tactility or Opticality, Henry Moore or David Smith: Herbert Read and Clement Greenberg on *The Art of Sculpture*, 1956', *Anglo-American Exchange in Postwar Sculpture, 1945–1975*: https://www.getty.edu/museum/symposia/pdf_stark/stark_getsy.pdf (accessed 7 March 2025).

13 Fiona Candlin (2010), *Art, Museums and Touch* (Manchester: Manchester University Press).

14 Oscar Holland, '4-year-old accidentally shatters Bronze Age jar at museum', *CNN*, 28 August 2024, https://www.cnn.com/2024/08/28/style/israel-haifa-museum-boy-breaks-artifact-hnk-intl/index.html (accessed 7 March 2025).

15 Julia Binswanger, 'This 4-Year-Old Shattered a Bronze Age Jar. Now, He'll Get to See How Experts Restored It', *Smithsonian Magazine*, 30 August 2024. https://www.smithsonianmag.com/smart-news/this-4-year-old-shattered-a-bronze-age-jar-now-hell-get-to-see-how-experts-restored-it-180984999/ (accessed 7 March 2025).

16 Plato (1963), *Greater Hippias*, in *The Collected Dialogues of Plato Including the Letters*, trans. Benjamin Jowett, ed. Edith Hamilton and Huntington Cairns (Princeton, NJ: Princeton University Press), 298a.

17 Aristotle (1987), 'Eudemian Ethics', trans. M. J. Woods, in *A New Aristotle Reader*, ed. J. L. Ackrill (Princeton, NJ: Princeton University Press), §1215b31–36.

18 Marsilio Ficino (1985), *Commentary on Plato's Symposium on Love*, trans. Sears Jayne (Dallas, TX: Spring Publications), 85–86.

19 Immanuel Kant (1987), *Critique of Judgment*, trans. Werner S. Pluhar (Indianapolis: Hackett), Part I, §9.

20 Immanuel Kant (2012), 'Lecture of the Winter Semester 1775–1776 based on the transcriptions Friedlander 3.3 (Ms 400), Friedlander 2 (Ms 399) and Prieger', trans. G. Felicitas Munzel, in *Lectures on*

Anthropology, edited by Robert B. Louden, 43–256 (Cambridge University Press), 25:496.

21 Kant, *Lectures on Anthropology*, 25:495–496.

22 Ibid., 25:296.

23 Ezgi Ucar, 'Multisensory Met: Touch, Smell, and Hear Art', The Met, 8 September 2015, https://www.metmuseum.org/articles/multisensory-met (accessed 7 March 2025).

24 Tiffany Field (2014), *Touch*, 2nd Edn. (Cambridge, MA: MIT Press), 14.

25 Mark Medley, 'Nick Bantock on the End of Griffin and Sabine's Epic Correspondence', *Globe and Mail*, 25 March 2016, https://www.theglobeandmail.com/arts/art-and-architecture/griffin-and-sabine-creator-nick-bantock-on-the-end-of-an-epic-correspondence/article29391999/ (accessed 7 March 2025).

26 Brenda Ross, 'Griffin and Sabine by Nick Bantock', *Info Cafe*, 20 October 2016, https://blogs.davenportlibrary.com/reference/griffin-and-sabine-by-nick-bantock/ (accessed 7 March 2025).

27 https://www.kicktraq.com/projects/1382819541/griffin-and-sabine-the-interactive-trilogy-by-nick/ (accessed 7 March 2025); Bound Press, "Kickstarter Campaign Announced for Nick Bantock, Griffin & Sabine App Trilogy', *PRWeb*, https://www.prweb.com/releases/kickstarter_campaign_announced_for_nick_bantock_griffin_sabine_app_trilogy/prweb12574897.htm (accessed 7 March 2025).

28 James Austin, '5 Offline Games We Love for Camping (That Are Also Great for the Backyard)', *New York Times*, 3 June 2024, https://www.nytimes.com/wirecutter/reviews/best-camping-backyard-games/ (accessed 7 March 2025). Austin also highlights the "clicky-clacky" pieces of another tile-placement game, *Hive Pocket*.

29 Jon Purkis, 'Top 10 Board Games to Play on Tabletop Simulator', *YouTube*, 23 April 2020, https://www.youtube.com/watch?v=JasuCclZ1v0 (accessed 7 March 2025).

30 Sega of America (1976) Promotional Brochure. https://www.pinrepair.com/arcade/fonz.htm (accessed 7 March 2025).

31 Daniel Martin, Sandra Malpica, Diego Gutierrez, Belen Masia, and Ana Serrano (2022), 'Multimodality in VR: A Survey', *ACM Computing Surveys* 54(10s): 216:1–216:36.

32 David Sax (2016), *The Revenge of Analog: Real Things and Why They Matter* (New York: PublicAffairs), 121.

33 Logan Hill, 'A Long Time Ago, in a Universe More Analog', *New York Times*, 27 October 2013, https://www.nytimes.com/2013/10/28/books/j-j-abrams-and-doug-dorst-collaborate-on-a-book-s.html (accessed 7 March 2025).

34 Alois Riegl (1996), 'The Modern Cult of Monuments: Its Essence and Its Development', trans. Karin Bruckner and Karen Williams, in Nicholas Stanley-Price, Mansfield Kirby Talley, and Alesandra Melucco Vaccaro, Alessandra, *Historical and Philosophical Issues in the Conservation of Cultural Heritage*, 69–83 (Los Angeles: Getty Conservation Institute).

35 Yuriko Saito (2007), *Everyday Aesthetics* (Oxford: Oxford University Press), 183.

36 Brandon Polite and Elizabeth Scarbrough (2025), 'Patina of Sound: Valuing Vinyl Records as Relics of Aged Interaction', *Espes* 14(1), 113.

37 Grant Peterson (2012), *Just Ride: A Radically Practical Guide to Riding Your Bike* (New York: Workman), 127.

38 Walter Benjamin (1968), 'The Work of Art in the Age of Mechanical Reproduction', trans. Harry Zohn, in *Illuminations*, 219–253 (New York: Harcourt), 222.

39 Ibid., 223.

40 See Andrew Kania (2006), 'Making Tracks: The Ontology of Rock Music', *Journal of Aesthetics and Art Criticism* 64(4), 401–414.

41 Albert Borgmann, *Technology and the Character of Contemporary Life*, 206.

42 Benjamin, 'The Work of Art in the Age of Mechanical Reproduction', 241.

3

The Value of Care

The King in Yellow

In February of 2020, Delaina and I heard that a local independent bookstore was closing. Joe's Place took up a large historic house near downtown Greenville, and books were spread throughout two floors. Coffee and wine served at the in-house cafe, and comfortable seating—both inside and on the long covered porch—made it a place to gather and linger. But the owners were ready to retire, and they were having an estate sale instead. Everything was for sale, from the books to the furniture to the wine bar. We heard about the sale late, and showed up on the last day. The shelves were pretty picked-over, but for a few bucks you could fill up a banker's box, so we wandered and picked. We found some nature books, some books by a local horror author, and a few other bits and bobs to fill out the box. When we got to the register, the woman in front of us was inquiring about buying the store's lighting fixtures, and the man running the checkout went off to examine the pieces in question, so we had some time to wait. While I held our place in line, Delaina started wandering the room. Directly across from the register—presumably where an employee could keep an eye on it—was a shelf of the expensive stuff. Delaina yelled out, "They've got a *King in Yellow*!"

Delaina is not exactly a hardcore horror fan, but she's married to one. I teach a course in the Philosophy of Horror, and *The King in Yellow* comes up early in the semester. Robert W. Chambers' book was written in the late nineteenth century, and has since developed a devoted cult following. Essentially, *The King in Yellow* is to horror enthusiasts what Tom Waits music is to musicians. It's not going to appeal to the casual horror reader (indeed, the casual horror reader won't likely have even heard of it), but devoted students of the genre—and especially of "weird" horror—gush over it, and it gets referenced a *lot* in horror stories, though usually in a subtle way—you have to know what to look for.* *The King in Yellow* is a collection of short stories, and I had several copies already, had read them many times, but Delaina carried over something I had only seen pictures of.

What Delaina handed me wasn't a first edition, published in 1895, but the much more iconic 1897 edition, instantly recognizable by the yellow-and-red angelic figure against the black cloth cover (some variation of which appears on most modern reprints). Since the man running the register was still off

---

*I was recently playing the game *Unspeakable Words* for the first time with some friends. It's a Cthulhu-themed spelling game, so there are a lot of references to H.P. Lovecraft's Old Gods. But part way through the game, to my delight, I drew a card called "The Yellow Sign"—a reference to Chambers' stories, but which made no explicit mention of *The King in Yellow*. IYKYK.

examining lighting fixtures, I had time to examine the book. It was *gorgeous*, in what seemed to be absolutely impeccable condition. The color on the cover—probably applied with a process called chromolithography—was bold and crisp. The silver ink used for the book's title looked like it couldn't have been shinier the day it was printed. The top edges of the paper were gilded gold, and still shone in the light. The only-slightly-off-white pages were bright and stiff, the edges sharp, the corners square. You could *see* how the text was stamped into the pages, the dents visible from the other side. You could *feel* them with your fingertips. An author's photograph on the fourth page was protected by a sheet of tissue paper, itself in perfectly crisp shape. You could barely smell the pages. In short, despite being more than a century old, this book did not look like it had ever been opened.

The price tag said $700. Premium items like this were excluded from the fill-a-box deal, of course. While I was fawning over it, the man returned, noticed my fawning, and said, "Make me an offer." I was a Visiting Assistant Professor at the time; my wife and I rented a house with a leaky roof. I certainly wasn't paying $700 for a book. I own a lot of books, but I'm not a book *collector* in the expensive sense. Even half the tagged price would have been a ridiculous expense for me. I said, despondently, "Any offer I can afford to make would be insulting," and moved to put it back on its shelf. But I suppose he must have seen the gleam in my eye, because he repeated, "Make me an offer," a little more firmly. So, I offered what I could legitimately justify spending, and which I knew he would turn down: "I could do fifty bucks."

"It's yours," he said. I was legitimately aghast.*

Now the book sits on its back on my horror bookshelf, behind glass, out of direct sunlight. I own plenty of books that I haven't read yet, but it's the only one I *know* I will never read.†

I feel a sort of *obligation* to maintain my copy of *The King in Yellow*, to keep it in as close to the condition in which I acquired it as I possibly can. This isn't because I plan to sell it some day—I don't. And although I think we may well have obligations to the dead, I don't see any reasonable argument that I owe any sort of obligation to Robert W. Chambers to keep his book in pristine condition. Nor do I see any argument that I owe such an obligation to the bookseller, despite his taking (or *because* he took) a mere $50 for the book. Indeed, I can't think of any person or persons to whom I would owe this obligation. Neither do I believe I owe any obligation to the object itself. Some would suggest that we have obligations to maintain cultural treasures, and that if I possess some such treasure, I have a sort of caretaker or stewardship obligation that I owe to the public at large.[1] But this seems unlikely in the present case. This is not the only copy of Chambers' book in existence, nor even the only copy of the 1897 edition. Indeed, there may well be other copies of the same edition in even better condition than mine. It would be difficult, then, to argue that this object is a cultural treasure in that sense.‡

*Standing there in line, I thought the $700 asking price was actually quite fair. Doing a little research now, I notice my copy is in *much* better condition than the copy currently being offered by a seller on AbeBooks for $1850.

†[Insert joke about never reading *The King in Yellow*. IYKYK.]

‡Erich Hatala Matthes makes a similar observation about Roman pottery in his 2024 book, *What to Save and Why: Identity, Authenticity, and the Ethics of Conservation*.

At the same time, I don't want to say that it would be merely a *shame* if the book managed to fall to pieces while in my collection. Rather, I want to say it would be a sort of personal failure—a failure to *care* properly. The value of caring—and its relevance to analog—is going to take some unpacking.

Analog and Care

James, a friend of mine in the neighborhood, holds monthly game nights in his house, hosting more than a dozen people some nights. Some of these are avid gamers, some are more occasional gamers, some are just looking for a night out. James is very generous with his games; although invitees are quite welcome to bring games to game nights, his library of 600+ games—surpassing the selection of some game stores—usually has whatever kind of game you might be looking to play. His e-mailed invitations to game nights, however, always include this line: "bring a game-friendly snack (so . . . not too greasy or sticky)." Although he very much wants to share the experience of these games, many are effectively irreplaceable, and are easily damaged or destroyed. Coasters are in plentiful supply at game nights. James points out that coasters give players a target for their drinks. Putting a card from a board game on the wet ring left by a sweaty glass can ruin that card—and often, thereby, the entire game. Some gamers use individual protective plastic sleeves for cards for exactly this sort of reason. James doesn't. Protective sleeves will do a lot to protect the cards, but they tend to make the games less playable.[*] So, instead, James just asks us to be careful—to care for his things as if they were your own. This is, of course, the irony of analog goods: much of their value is realized in their use, but their use inevitably degrades them. If they degrade too much, or in the wrong ways, we can't use them anymore. Fragile books are difficult to read. Scratched records and games with missing components are difficult to play. Jigsaw puzzles missing pieces, meanwhile, should be consigned to the flames.

The sort of analog objects I have in mind are often *notoriously* fragile. A slight slip of a thumb in handling a vinyl record can result in an irreparable scratch from a thumbnail. Accepted wisdom among record collectors is that vinyl should be stored upright, lest albums warp or (in extreme cases) crack from the pressure of records stacked atop them.[†] Album covers made of rigid cardboard help to prevent warping from heat, and paper record sleeves inside these help to minimize the damage of sliding records into and out of their cardboard jackets, to keep static and dust from accumulating on the vinyl, and to protect records from acid in the cardboard that will slowly wear away at the surface of an album. They're like paper tighty-whities, and Delaina and I buy them in bulk.

---

[*]Asked why he doesn't sleeve his cards, James says, "Well, my games tend not to get played so much that I'm worried about damaging them through use. And I kind of like the look they get from wear when they *have* been played a lot." Beausage.

[†]There's a scene in the 2000 film *High Fidelity* where the socially awkward Dick comes across his boss, Rob, reorganizing his vinyl collection. Rob is surrounded by stacks of records, and Dick says, "You really shouldn't keep them piled like this, because it gets really pressured, y'know." Telling a vinylphile like Rob about the dangers of stacking records is like telling him what a spindle adaptor is for.

Acid is also a problem for anything made of paper, including comic books, magazines, and print books—particularly cheap paperbacks. For a very long time, comics were published on cheap newsprint, which is acid-heavy, turning pages yellow and brittle over time, and which is prone to tearing, pages easily pulling from the staples along the spine.* The same acid problem threatens old paperbacks, and cheap glue binding tends to come apart through use, or degrades from heat and sun exposure.

Water is bad for pretty much everything.

Analog film, meanwhile, is an absolute nightmare. Prior to exposure, it needs to be stored in absolute darkness in a dry, temperature-stable environment—ideally a refrigerator. But even in these conditions, unused film won't last forever. The cocktail of chemicals used to treat film deteriorates over time—a couple of years at room temperature, longer if colder. Older films that used nitrate have a tendency to spontaneously combust.

Analog goods are—by their nature—things that need to be cared for, and which illustrate on their surface whether they *have* been cared for. Still, care for analog goods may feel a tad strange

---

*But also producing that delightful smell we talked about last chapter. While my copy of *The King in Yellow* sits on that shelf, safely outside the corrosive touch of sunlight, directly above it, in the attic, are my old boxes of comic books, which I have been amassing since I was 11 years old. Most of these comics are in terrible shape, some read and re-read to tatters, falling apart at the seams like the Velveteen Rabbit. Other comic-book collectors take very good care of their collections, and there is an industry based on preserving such delicate goods. For a fee, the Certified Guaranty Company (CGC) in Sarasota, Florida, will assess the condition of your comic book, assign it a numeric grade up to 10, and seal the comic in an airtight plastic package—a process known as "slabbing." Opening that package invalidates the grading, so slabbing puts the comic forever out of touch.

in today's world. We live in a consumer society that demands we continue to consume. How many iPods, iPads, and iPhones have I cared for only to be informed that the thing I put in a protective case, covered in scratch-proof glass, and successfully refrained from dropping in a toilet, is now obsolete, will no longer be supported by Apple, and is now only useful as landfill?

Yuriko Saito notes, "One reason [for the overflow of manufactured goods in our lives] is the overabundance of relatively inexpensive consumer goods which encourages us to treat various objects as disposables because replacement is easy to come by."[2] On one philosophy, an object needn't last any longer than the trend that gave rise to it. If someone is only going to replace that good with the next shiny thing, why put the expense into making the good last any longer than that? This is the philosophy behind "fast fashion"—clothing churned out to meet the fashionable demand, but of cheap materials that may be discarded when the fad moves on.*

Much of the analog stuff I'm talking about in this book was designed to be disposable—not because it was easily replaced, but because it was *consumable*. The reason that rare comic books *are* so rare is that they were intended to be thrown out like yesterday's newspaper, so they weren't designed to last. It was

*That fast fashion is aimed primarily at women is quickly illustrated by a trip to Goodwill, where the floorspace devoted to women's clothing invariably and dramatically outweighs that of men's clothing. Men tend to hold onto their clothes and drive them into the ground, so what little men's clothes you'll find are often wildly out of fashion. Moreover, men's clothing is usually built to last, a value that men tend to have in their garments.

their disposability then that led to their collectability today. In April of 2024, a copy of the first issue of *The Avengers* sold at auction for $432,000, a rather sizeable increase from the 12-cent cover price it had when it hit newsstands in 1963.[3] Copies of comics from that era or earlier are extremely scarce specifically because they were designed to be consumed and discarded, and this particular copy was still in like-new condition (indeed, probably better condition than a copy you would find on a pharmacy spinner-rack in 1963).*

Digital goods are perhaps the most easily replaced of all. Where analog goods are often scarce, going out of print and becoming difficult and expensive to replace, digital files are copied quickly and without loss. I can just store all of my files in the Cloud, and pull them onto my devices whenever I like. If I'm going on a road trip where I expect only intermittent signal, I will download an array of songs or podcasts to my phone so that I can enjoy them whenever I like, deleting them from my phone just as easily after I arrive. I maintain subscriptions for Microsoft Office and the Adobe Creative Suite, so that whenever I get a new device, I can simply download the same programs again. All of this, of course, is right in line with the ease and efficiency we value in digital goods. I don't really *have* to care for digital goods

---

*Now that comics have gained "collectability" status, they are published on glossy acid-free paper. The cover price of a typical comic book in 1991 was one US dollar. Today, it is four times that, nearly doubling the standard rate of inflation (https://www.comichron.com/vitalstatistics/mediancoverprices.html). Comics in the past were cheap because they were designed to be disposable; new ones are expensive today because they are designed to be collected.

because they are intangible. An individual copy of a file might become corrupted for any number of reasons, but as long as I have a backup, I probably have little to worry about. Without that perceived fragility, the nature of digital goods simply does not breed the same attitude of care as does that of their analog equivalents.* When I take care of a book or a record or a board game, I am preserving an *individual thing*, and caring for a thing creates a relationship. Once upon a time—really, not that long ago—digital goods came on physical media that needed to be cared for: floppy disks, game cartridges, CDs, DVDs. But in this era of streaming, physical media has become antiquated. In most cases, there really isn't a *thing* to care for anymore.

Care as a Virtue

In philosophy, the topic of care comes up most often in the field of ethics, particularly as it arises from the field of virtue ethics. Virtue ethics is the granddaddy of moral theories. Here in the West, virtue ethics is most famously anchored in the work

*There are some exceptions. I talked last chapter about the storage of digital masters for recordings. As well, there is a small industry devoted to preserving and repairing original Nintendo game cartridges, despite those same games being available to play in emulators. Video game enthusiasts are as susceptible to sentimental fetishism as anybody else. (My thanks to Chris Alvin for pointing this out.) The National Museum of American History, part of the Smithsonian Institution, maintains a collection of video games and video game systems, including a mangled cartridge of the Atari 2600 game, *E.T.: The Extraterrestrial*, excavated from a landfill where Atari buried millions of overstock cartridges in 1983.

of Aristotle—particularly his *Nicomachean Ethics*—though his teacher Plato espoused a virtue-ethical approach, as did *his* teacher, Socrates.* Meanwhile, in the East, virtue-based approaches had flourished long before Aristotle happened along, and continued to flourish for centuries afterwards.† Virtue ethics was eventually sidelined by new ethical models emerging in the Enlightenment, including utilitarianism and deontology, and became a sort of also-ran in philosophy classrooms. But the classical approach was roused from its slumber in the mid-twentieth century, and has been steadily regaining ground ever since.

Virtue ethics is centrally concerned with "the good," and for the virtue ethicist, two questions are intertwined: what does it mean to be a good *person*, and what does it mean to live a good *life*? Where utilitarians would locate goodness in the predictable outcome of an action, and deontologists would locate goodness in the will of the person performing the action, virtue ethicists locate goodness in a person's character.‡ Rather than asking,

---

*Socrates didn't write anything down, so much of what we know about Socrates' own ideas comes from his students, particularly Plato, who employed his teacher as a central figure in most of his dialogues. Unfortunately, it can be difficult to know at times where Socrates' ideas end and Plato's begin. Fortunately, another of Socrates' students, Xenophon, also wrote dialogues featuring his teacher, and which tend to be treated as having more historical veracity (if only because he seems to have less imagination). Both Plato's Socrates and Xenophon's talk about virtue.

†The *Analects*, a collection of sayings attributed to Confucius, who lived more than a century before Aristotle, includes several passages outlining a virtue ethic.

‡I am neither presenting nor endorsing any particular fine-grained virtue theory. In what follows in this section, I will be making some broad blanket statements about virtue ethics. For each such statement, I expect there will be at least one person who self-identifies as a virtue theorist who will reject that statement. Such is the nature of philosophy.

"what should I do?", virtue ethics asks, "what kind of person should I be?" and "how do I get there?" Virtuous actions will thereafter take care of themselves.

Developing the virtues is a lifelong process, but we start with the idea that we can usually identify the virtues without much difficulty. Patience is a virtue. Courage is a virtue. We tend to know the virtues when we see them, even if we couldn't explain exactly what it is that makes *this* particular behavior patient (rather than merely passive) or courageous (rather than foolhardy). In general, virtue ethicists agree that any virtue is a sort of disposition to *respond well.* What distinguishes one virtue from another is the class of things being responded to. A person with patience responds well to impediments to their goals; a person with courage responds well in the face of danger. And care, I want to say, is a response to perceived fragility and value.

The closest that Aristotle himself seems to get to dealing with care is in a broader discussion of friendship. The relevant Greek word he uses is *philēsis,* usually translated as "love" or "friendly feeling." Aristotle notes that someone might feel *philēsis* towards some inanimate object, like a board game.* But, Aristotle says, *true friendship* (being a virtue) is not a mere feeling; friendship

*Aristotle doesn't actually give an example, but both Plato and Aristotle mention *petteia* in their writings—a family of abstract strategy games involving a board and stones—so we might imagine Aristotle thinking here of his affinity for his game set, a gift from his teacher. Aristotle talks about *petteia* in his *Politics* (1253a), and Plato in the *Republic* (487b). Since Plato handed his Academy over to his nephew, Speusippus, however, rather than to his star pupil, Aristotle (who then went off to form his own school), I have no particular reason to think that Plato would have given Aristotle a *petteia* set, nor that Aristotle would have thought fondly of such a gift.

involves *choice*, and choice "springs from a state of character."[4] So, while that game I own may evoke a warm feeling in me, friendship is more than a warm feeling. Friendship involves active participation in a relationship. Now, I wouldn't suggest that the sort of care I direct towards a board game, vinyl record, or comic book is a relationship like friendship, neither do I think of care as a mere friendly feeling. Care is an active engagement, not a passive affect.

On the classic account from Aristotle, for an action to be virtuous, it must arise in the right sort of way. It cannot be the *mere* emulation of behavior. Acting virtuously requires the right intention and the right knowledge, and must arise from a firm and steady character.[5]

The *right intention* involves choosing the action for its own sake, and not for some external reward. Certainly, much of the care that I direct towards the analog goods in my possession is at least partly selfishly motivated: I want to be able to continue to enjoy these things. But, I think, this is not all. On occasion, Delaina and I downsize our collections. About once a year, we reconsider our book collections, pulling out those volumes we are unlikely to want to read again. We regularly replay our board games to decide if we still want to keep them. And we are currently listening to every one of our several hundred vinyl albums—in order—to decide if each should be kept or passed on. We are almost always amassing a box for Goodwill.

When we do cast off parts of our collections, having already decided we won't be enjoying them again in the future, the urge does not arise to treat these books, games, and records with any less care than we had so far been treating them. Certainly, we donate such items to Goodwill or otherwise pass them along with the hope that someone else will get some enjoyment from them. But the thought of taking a box cutter to an album, simply emptying a game box into the trash, or throwing a book on the fire produces an immediate wave of revulsion in me.* It is not merely that such actions would be *wasteful*, but that they would be *wanton*. Consider again my copy of *The King in Yellow*: I am never going to read it (and would keep it out of the hands of anyone who said they would), and I am never going to sell it. Neither my wife nor any other member of my family has any interest in inheriting it, should I get hit by a bus. I am not caring for it for any selfish reason that I can identify. Rather, I think, I am caring for it because *it is a thing to be cared for*, the same reason that we plucked our most recent kitten out of a ditch when she was the size of a hot dog bun, and a thunderstorm was threatening. To repeat: care is a response to perceived fragility and value.

When Delaina and I started collecting records, it was on a lark. A friend was having a birthday party, and set up his garage as a smashing room. Everybody was instructed to bring things they wanted to destroy. I tried to think of the most fragile and disposable things I could, and I came up with vinyl records and teacups—neither of which I owned, but both of which were in abundant and cheap supply at thrift stores. I figured we could

*Again, jigsaw puzzles with missing pieces should always be burned, and doing so always engenders a positive feeling.

throw one at the other. Knowing this was the plan, we refused to spend more than 50 cents on a record, and picked the ones with the most ridiculous covers. As the date of the party approached, however, Delaina declared that we couldn't simply destroy the records without listening to them, so she bought a used suitcase-style Crosley turntable—the kind you see on the shelf for $50 or $60 at Target. And, it turns out, three of the records were things that it felt, well, *wrong* to destroy. They were things of value.

As our collection grew, several people told us—in no uncertain terms—that we were destroying our records with our Crosley. Although Crosley does make higher-end turntables, the cheap ones (like ours) don't have counterweights for the arm that holds the needle, so the tip is resting lightly on the record itself. The concern is that, without the counterweight, that needle is *dragging* through the vinyl, damaging it a little more with each spin of the record. Those Crosley turntables did a lot for reinvigorating vinyl, but they aren't doing a lot for your records, it seems.* When we replied that we rarely spent more than 50 cents on a record, their objections tended to soften. Damaging a thing already considered of low value was not serious loss. Still, as our collection grew, we decided to up our turntable game.

Delaina wanted a turntable that you could stack several records on, so that when one record ended, the next one would drop on top of it and start playing. I remembered my parents having one of these in a cabinet roughly the size of a station wagon; we were hoping for something a little more streamlined.

---

*There is some debate about this among enthusiasts.

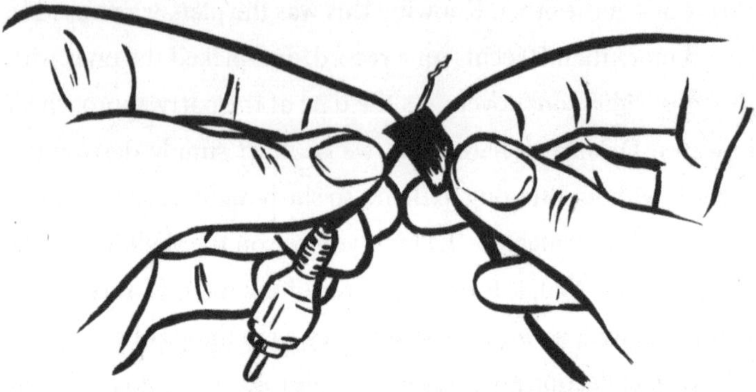

The problem, it turns out, is that this sort of turntable—called a record changer—hasn't been manufactured by anyone since 1993. If we wanted a record changer, we had to buy vintage. Happily, we discovered, there is a vintage audio shop in town run as a sort of hobby by the owner, where we found a "pristine" 1970s Dual 1237 turntable with a record changer. It was exactly what we wanted. We tested it in the shop, and it worked great. We paid $300, and drove the two miles home, Delaina holding the turntable on her lap like a newborn baby. We set it up, plugged it in, and audio only came through the right speaker. We tried everything we could think of—everything within our skillset—including Delaina repatching two RCA cables hardwired into the machine, but we ultimately had to give up and bring the turntable back to the store. It turns out that some bit of wiring in the cartridge (the part that holds the needle) had come loose and was quickly fixed by the owner of the store. So, we brought our vintage baby home again, set it up, plugged it in, and the audio problem was solved. But now the automatic return on the arm wasn't working, so back to the store we went. The owner, who had made it clear from the beginning that all sales were final and that he did not take returns, told us that he wasn't going to repair the turntable again, but would take it back and return our money. The message was pretty clear: we didn't have the sort of basic knowledge required to care for this machine, and it needed to be taken away from us. Care is not simply an attitude; it requires the *right knowledge*. In this case, the requisite knowledge was of a sort that takes education and practice, and learning what we needed to know on that vintage turntable would have been like learning gross anatomy on fragile but healthy live patients. We lacked what Aristotle would call *phrónēsis*—practical wisdom: the necessary knowledge to turn our virtuous attitude into virtuous action. The shop owner's caring didn't end when that Dual 1237 left his store, and the idea of putting it in the hands of a couple of well-meaning but unskilled enthusiasts was enough for him to make an exception to his all-sales-are-final policy, to ensure its continued care. Caring is not an individual act, but an ongoing relationship, which is why it's hard to let go of what we have cared for.

Some virtue ethicists may insist that care, as a virtue, is the sort of thing that is directed primarily and properly towards persons, and not towards mere things. As virtue theory sprung renewed in the garden of ethics, it sent out a new shoot in the form of *care ethics*. Care ethics is almost entirely about caring between persons, and care ethicists may balk at the notion of equivocating care for persons and care for objects. Nel Noddings, one of the progenitors of the field of care ethics, is also one of the few to raise the question of how care ethics might extend beyond care relationships with other people. She notes that "many of us experience in our encounters with animals feelings very much like those we are familiar with in genuinely ethical situations."[6] The same, I expect, is true of those nonliving things we care for. Noddings' view is that we care for each other because *we* were cared for. But, Noddings argues, "our obligation to summon the caring attitude is limited by the possibility of reciprocity."[7] If the object of our caring attitude cannot reciprocate, then we have no such obligation to care for it. And while my cats cannot care for me as I care for them, I nevertheless have a two-way relationship with them. I know how each responds to my care actions, and each has its own way of letting me know what it wants. (Every cat I have owned has figured out its own way to wake me up in the morning.) My cats know they are loved. As a result of this kind of relationship with my cats, Noddings says, I incur obligations to consider their welfare. Plants, on the other hand, respond to my care*taking*—to the water, heat, and sunlight I provide—but not my *caring*, and would flourish just as well if there was a machine providing for them. So, Noddings says, "I shall not be pleased if you kill the plant I give you, but I cannot pass an ethical judgment on you."[8] Mere *things*, she suggests, have passed so far outside the ethical sphere as to merit mentioning them only to dismiss them: "My main reason for setting things aside is that we behave ethically only through them and not toward them."[9] *My* interests, however, are not about *ethics* so much as they are about *values*, insofar as we can make any clear distinction here. Perhaps

I have no *obligations* to mere things, but I certainly *value* them, and I value their care.

Whether or not I have an *obligation* to care for it, allowing my copy of *The King in Yellow* to fall to pieces while in my possession feels like a fault in my *character*. Virtues are character traits and aren't simply directed towards some particular object. A courageous person isn't courageous only with regard to lions, or only with regard to dentistry. A modest person is not merely modest with regard to their academic accomplishments, or only with regard to their natural gifts. The same, I would say, is true of the virtue of care. Someone who demonstrates the appropriate level of care towards their books (things, that is, that they recognize as vulnerable and valuable) is more likely to do the same for their plants, their pets, and their friends. Care involves the conscientious consideration and treatment of a vulnerable thing that won't last forever. One might think that the value of care is that it is good *practice* for caring for a human, like we tell somebody who wants to be a parent to try a pet first. But care in all its forms connects with deliberateness and conscientiousness, which are valuable in themselves.

Care and the Individual

While the deontologist and the utilitarian offer us systems for assessing particular actions, their focus is on general abstract rules that would apply to any scenario: figuring out the abstract principle is the primary task; applying it to particular cases is a secondary and largely mechanical matter. Conversely, while care is a disposition—a sort of *general* way of being—care itself is always grounded in relationships with *individuals*. It is at least partly for this reason that care ethics has made such inroads in the medical field. While I might not expect (or, indeed, even want) a legislator to get involved in the lives of every one of her constituents, I very much want my doctors to treat me as an individual person with my own history, concerns, and values.* Similarly, we would find it at least odd—and perhaps repellant—for a parent to care for their child according to the dictates of a general rule, rather than for the individual that child is.[10]

Last chapter, we talked about materiality and individuality. As with materiality, care *requires* attending to the individual, whether that's a person, a pet, or a vinyl record.[11] I don't have a *care* relationship with a song (say, The Who's "Magic Bus"), nor with the album it appears on (*Meaty Beaty Big and Bouncy*).† We don't generally *care* for abstract things: because we don't see them as fragile, care isn't called for.‡ There is little I can do to damage the thing that The Who made. But I *do* have a care relationship with my particular *copy* of that album, which *is* a thing that can be easily damaged, and so I treat it in a particular way.

---

*And I have certainly been attended to by doctors who were more interested in efficiency than care.

†Yes, "Magic Bus" first appeared as a single, and then on *Magic Bus: The Who on Tour*, three years before 1971's *Meaty Beaty Big and Bouncy*, but I don't own either of those albums, and have no care relationship with them.

‡Democracy is an exception—we care for it both because we see it as valuable, and because we see it as fragile.

We don't aim care at everything in our lives, nor everything in our homes, even when we perceive them as fragile and valuable. The attitude of care is inevitably selective, aimed at things with individual perceived value. With an object like an heirloom or a souvenir, where the object comes into our lives already endowed with special significance, we may be more inclined to give it special attention and care. Ordinary analog objects like board games or books don't tend to come into our lives in particularly significant ways, and so they are usually not immediately endowed with that special significance. Although we might occasionally stumble across a gem like an 1897 edition of *The King in Yellow*, in most cases, I suspect, we *come to singularize* the objects as we handle and care for them. *That* object comes to mean something, not simply as a copy of an album or a story, but as a thing-in-itself. Some of this singularity will be apparent in the age value and beausage that these objects take on through use, and some will be invisible, arising from our personal association with the objects in our care. The album or the comic book becomes less replaceable because our caring *makes them singular*—our caring enhances their aura. The overlap here with the value of materiality and its association with individuality should not be surprising: my care is a hands-on sort of thing, and I can't get my hands on what I can't get my hands on.

Care involves a special attitude, and there is a longstanding view in the philosophy of art that properly appreciating art requires a special attitude, too. The hallmark of this "aesthetic attitude" is that it is appropriately *distanced*. In the eighteenth century, this was dubbed *disinterestedness*, and was meant to apply to *all* aesthetic appreciation, whether of art or of nature. The idea is that our personal associations tend to cloud our judgments. The hiker who pauses to appreciate the beauty of a valley she passes through will engage an altogether different sort of appreciation than the landowner, who cultivates and eats from the same valley. Likewise for the viewer who is appreciating a painting for art's sake, and another who is wondering how it would look hanging above the sofa. When there's a personal stake in it, the idea goes, our appreciation is not going to be purely aesthetic, but muddied with the subjective and the practical. Ideally, to properly appreciate the painting or the natural landscape before me, I should have no personal stake in it. Lord Shaftesbury,* who first introduced the idea, suggests that aesthetic appreciation is a sort of *intellectual* satisfaction, distinct from *sensual* satisfaction or *practical* concerns tied up with ownership.[12] Rather than appreciating the particular before me, the thinking goes, I should be appreciating the abstract form that it embodies—seeing *through* the particular *to* the universal.† Immanuel Kant goes even further to suggest

*Sir Anthony Ashley Cooper, Third Earl of Shaftesbury, simply referred to by scholars in the field as "Shaftesbury."

†Notice that this approach to aesthetics, like the theories of utilitarianism and deontology developed around the same time, promote the universal, abstract, and general over the particular and individual. Last chapter, we discussed the prioritization of sight and sound, over touch, taste and smell—the former being intellectual, the latter animalistic. Shaftesbury makes the same distinction here: as "brutes" can appreciate the sensuousness of the particular, it must be the abstract, appreciable through the organs of intellect, that should appeal to man and give rise to the higher pleasures.

that proper aesthetic appreciation excludes even concern for the object's actual *existence.*[13]

While most of the analog goods I have been talking about fall broadly under the heading of "art," the notion of disinterest seems obviously at odds with the idea of a care relationship with the sorts of analog objects we have been discussing. First, caring necessarily aims *at* the individual rather than *past* the individual to something abstract, general, or universal. Second, the care attitude is necessarily subjective, depending upon the value judgments of the individual judge. And, third, as engagement with analog objects is irreducibly multimodal, separating our intellectual from our sensual engagement with them feels artificial—feels *weird*. That such a line is drawn in a normative color gives the whole enterprise an off-putting atmosphere of Levitical "purity."

In the twentieth century, philosophers began to question the line that had long been drawn between the aesthetic and the practical, and of isolating art objects from the real-world fabric of our lives. One of the founders of American pragmatism, John Dewey, suggested that those experiences we want to call aesthetic are characterized instead by the focus and flow of those experiences: "the work of art develops and accentuates what is characteristically valuable in things of everyday enjoyment."[14] On Dewey's view, the experience of artworks isn't special because they have a value foreign to our ordinary lives, but because it is in our experiences of them that we find our values intersecting, and our focus enhances and particularizes those experiences, and particularizes those objects.

The Experience of Care

Dewey admits that the sort of aesthetic experience he describes is rare. He suggests that such an experience must be unified, internally coherent, and intense in a way that most of our experiences simply aren't. Dewey as such distinguishes between "mere" experience—a drifting sort of thing with nothing to hold it all together—and "an" experience, which may be properly described as "aesthetic." A newer movement in "everyday aesthetics" suggests, in contrast, that aesthetic experience is all around us. Sherri Irvin argues that our everyday lives are *rich* with aesthetic potential—that "our everyday lives have an aesthetic character that is thoroughgoing and available at every moment, should we choose to attend to it."[15] Much of this aesthetic potential drifts past us as we flow through the stream of our daily lives. But, Irvin notes:

> there is the possibility of bringing many things that are currently unconsciously undergone into consciousness, something that is advocated by many forms of meditative practice: it is possible for me to attend to the feelings of my fingers on the keyboard as I type, although I usually fail to do so.[16]

I usually fail to do so, because when I'm typing away on my keyboard (as I am at this very moment), I am usually involved in a task, and that task has an end-goal. Attending to the feeling of my fingers and the keyboard as I pluck away at the keys means shifting my focus away from that goal. That shifting of attention, I find, is actually surprisingly easy to do; it's *maintaining* that attention that's hard, as the original goal continually calls my attention back.

Irvin's choice of attending to the feeling of fingers on a keyboard is interesting. Certainly, I *can* attend to my digital devices in a way that Irvin would call aesthetic.* I *can* attend to the very light buzzing produced by my computer monitor, and which I usually ignore. I *can* attend to the quality of light

---

*There is some debate in the field of everyday aesthetics about whether the ordinary must be elevated to the extraordinary in order to be properly characterized as aesthetic. Thomas Leddy says yes, appropriating Benjamin's flexible notion of "aura" to mean "the quality of heightened significance" (Leddy, *The Extraordinary in the Ordinary*, 116), to say, "Only when something has aura can it be said to have an aesthetic property." (135) Yuriko Saito says no: "I locate the core of everyday aesthetics in the ordinary experienced as ordinary: the quiet, unarticulated aesthetic satisfaction interwoven with the flow of daily life" (Saito, *The Aesthetics of the Familiar*, 124). The humdrum can be experienced as aesthetic without having to elevate it from the ordinary to the extraordinary. Truthfully, I am less concerned with whether these experiences are properly described as "aesthetic" than whether they are *valuable*.

produced by my phone, but I usually don't. I *can* attend to the feeling of the earbuds in my ears, but, again, I usually don't. The difference between my experience of most things digital and most things analog is that the sensory qualities that I *could* attend to with digital devices are typically antithetical to the reason I am dealing with the digital in the first place. Earbuds are supposed to be so comfortable that you forget they are even there. A monitor that emits even a light buzzing sound is a problem. Computer monitors, televisions, and speakers are all marketed for their *clarity*: as things to be experienced *through*, not to be experienced themselves. Such concerns, however, don't tend to tread on the analog. The smell of old comics, the heft of a board game, and the feel of type pressed into the pages of *The King in Yellow* are all aesthetic qualities that enrich my experiences without problematically detracting from those same experiences. Where the value of efficiency built into so much of our lives—and in particular with anything digital—aims us at some end goal, analog provides a respite from ends-oriented intention. Digital technology's focus on efficiency leans into an attitude of *hurrying up*. But the care demanded of analog requires *slowing down*.

The multimodal richness offered by analog objects provides opportunities for *dwelling* in their aesthetic richness, and the care that analog objects require has a way of maximizing our attention. Caring for my objects *requires* slowing down and being attentive. It's precisely when you're rushing or are distracted that a record gets scratched, a comic gets torn, or a game card gets set in the puddle left on the table by a cold glass. It's in slowing down and attending to analog objects that I get to dwell in their multimodal richness. The analog promotes care, and care promotes attentiveness—slowing down, being in the moment.[17]

On the subject of care, Irvin's mention of "meditative practice" points us in a fruitful direction. In Robert Pirsig's classic novel, *Zen and the Art of Motorcycle Maintenance*, the narrator talks about the experience of care, in particular as experienced by a mechanic or machinist: "They have patience, care and attentiveness to what they're doing, but more than this . . . there's a kind of inner peace of mind that isn't contrived but results from a kind of harmony with the work in which there's no leader and no follower."[18] Peace of mind comes with being in the moment.* The Zen approach promotes mindfulness, and the mindful mechanic isn't simply looking for the most efficient way to get the job done.† He is fully present in the moment. With

---

*Albert Borgmann interprets the book as offering this lesson: "To attain harmony with technology . . . we must take up the practice of maintaining and caring for the technological objects about us" (Borgmann, *Technology and the Character of Contemporary Life*, 161).

†Earlier in the book, the narrator talks about his experience of trying to identify a persistent problem with his motorcycle, which kept seizing up at high speeds. The narrator brought the bike to a shop, where the mechanics first pre-identified the problem—in error—and then replaced a series of engine parts to no avail, ultimately causing more problems than they solved. The seizing continued. It wasn't until the narrator took the engine apart himself that he found the problem: a sheared pin was preventing oil from reaching the engine at high speeds. The narrator reflects . . . "I don't want to hurry it. That itself is a poisonous twentieth-century attitude. When you want to hurry something, that means you no longer care about it and want to get on to other things. I just want to get at it slowly, but carefully and thoroughly, with the same attitude I remember was present just before I found that sheared pin. It was that attitude that found it, nothing else" (35).

appropriate mindfulness, *care is a felt phenomenon*. Practitioners describe it as a sort of calm attentiveness.

I can find the same sort of peace in simply cleaning the dust from a record. I'm not in a rush; I'm enjoying this moment. Rather than the aesthetic distance that Shaftesbury and Kant called for, I am *present* in the activity, mindful of the weight and the fragility of the vinyl, the sharpness of the edge as I hold it with my thumb, the smoothness of the vinyl as my brush glides over its surface. I remain in the moment as I carefully set the record on the turntable spindle and set the needle onto the spinning vinyl, waiting for that first crackle as the needle finds the groove.

The fact that I have done this hundreds upon hundreds of times does not breed carelessness. Yuriko Saito says something similar about participants in the Japanese tea ceremony: "Although highly prescribed and choreographed and requiring repeated practice, the slow and elegant body movements of the host making tea and the guest receiving and savoring the drink are a silent but eloquent expression of the care and respect for the other party."[19] When we care for other people, we get a sense of purpose, a sense of renewal, a *reason* to slow down and be considerate. I want to say that we get the same when we care for animals, or plants, or machines, or just . . . stuff. Archivists Michelle Caswell and Marika Cifor write, "Care includes both the often bodily labours of providing what is necessary for the health, sustainment, and protection of someone or something, and the feeling of concern and attachment that provokes such acts."[20] Even where the object of care is a vinyl record, a turntable, a typewriter, or a book, care breeds mindfulness.

Indeed, there is something of a surprising movement in "mindful" or "meditative" cleaning. Leo Babauta writes,

> I wipe a counter with a rag, but I'm not doing it thinking, "This kitchen is so dirty!" (judgment) or "I wish people would clean up after themselves!" (expecting things to be different) or "I have a lot of work to do today" (future thinking) or "My son really got on my nerves when he said that this morning" (dwelling on the past). Or at least, when I do think these things, I notice them, and return to the wiping.
>
> As I wipe the counter, I notice the crumbs and dried spilled liquid. I feel the rag going over the bumpy surface of the counter, and gradually feel the surface smoothing out. I feel the tension in my shoulders and jaw, and relax them. I become aware of my breath as it comes in and goes out. I rinse the rag out carefully, cleaning it and watching the dirty water run down the drain.[21]

John P. Miller, scholar of holistic education, talks about the experience of mindful care in simply cleaning up at the end of the day:

> After the children have left, I sweep the floor, being mindful of my movements and the sound of the broom. I often begin by thinking that I am sweeping the day's events away and that I am focusing on the "now" – the actual act of sweeping. The pleasure of being here, and being able to fully participate reminds me again of the miracle of life.[22]

At the end of the day, with all pressing tasks completed, there is opportunity to be in the moment, and to fully experience what that moment (and so life in general) has to offer.*

Perhaps surprisingly, there appears to be little empirical research on the psychological effects of cleaning, or of caring for analog goods. There is, however, a body of such research on care when it comes to *plants*.

In a 2015 study in the *Journal of Physiological Anthropology*, researchers studied the comparative effects of engaging in a simple digital activity (preparing a document on a laptop) and a simple gardening activity (transporting indoor plants to larger pots).[23] While those engaged in the digital activity showed increased stress levels during the task and higher blood pressure at its conclusion, those engaged in the gardening activity showed continually decreasing stress levels through the activity and lower blood pressure afterwards. Where those engaged in the digital activity reported discomfort and agitation, those caring for the plants reported feeling more soothed and comfortable. On the scale provided to participants in the study, the opposite

---

*Advocates of mindful cleaning offer several tips that apply nicely to caring for analog objects, including:

(1) Be present. Focus on the present moment and the sensation you're taking in.
(2) Don't clean to have a clean thing. Rather, clean to clean. Focus on process rather than outcome.
(3) Take your time.

Much of this approach to mindfulness is couched in terms of Zen philosophy, but (unlike Babauta and Miller) isn't coming from Zen practitioners. (See, e.g. Eisler's "Mindful Cleaning Practice," Ahmen Mezil's "The Art of Mindful Cleaning," and A La Maid's "Zen and the Art of Meditative Cleaning.")

of "soothing" was "awakening," which seems like a strange pairing. And, indeed, in a 2018 study that effectively replicated both the 2015 experiment and its outcomes, subjects performing the gardening activity also showed increased alpha brainwave activity compared with those performing the digital activity, noting that increased alpha waves are associated with relaxation, happiness, and wakefulness.[24] Though the digital activity was a familiar kind of task for participants, being university students, and the gardening task involved learning new skills, the former built stress and the latter reduced it. All of this sounds right in line with the experiences described by practitioners of mindful cleaning.

Empirical research has not been limited to individual plant care activities. Several studies have looked at the long-term effects of caring for house plants, typically in aging adults. Two classic studies by Ellen J. Langer and Judith Rodin compared outcomes for nursing home residents, one group being given houseplants to care for, and another given plants that the staff would care for. Participants were initially studied over three weeks. Those taking care of the plants themselves reported significantly increased happiness and feelings of activity compared with the control group, and independent observation by the nursing home's medical staff reported that 93% of the first group showed overall health improvement compared with only 21% of the control.[25] Eighteen months later, Langer and Rodin revisited the same nursing home, and found that while the death rate across those caring for their plants was 15%, the death rate for the control group was 30%.[26] Now, the idea that caring for houseplants might have such a measurable health outcome may sound preposterous, but empirical research continues to point in this direction.

In a 2018 study, seniors recovering from hip fractures were shown to have faster recovery over the first six months if they were caregivers (whether of plants, pets, or other persons) than if they were non-caregivers, and *in particular* if they cared for plants. As my colleague Sarah points out, caring for people and pets is *work*; caring for plants is "just caring." And, as the authors of the study suggest, "it is likely that the engagement in caregiving itself and not the type of plant was related to the beneficial impact on functional recovery after hip fracture."[27]

Earlier this chapter, I noted that plants respond to our caretaking. Apparently, *we also* respond to our caretaking for plants. And, while our plants would do just as well if a machine took care of them, we apparently would not, for there is something important in the caretaking itself—both in the individual *acts* of caretaking, and in the ongoing *role* as a caretaker. And, as all of this seems to be the case regardless of what it is that is being cared for, taking care of analog goods should serve just as well. Caring is caring.

Caring about Care

Of course, care activities aren't always going to be meditative. Sometimes that value of efficiency takes precedence. Sometimes I've got somewhere to be. Sometimes company is coming over.

But the analog allows for these experiences in a way that the digital generally does not, offering an oasis from the increasingly multitasking digital world where I am expected to be available by cell phone at any time. Slowing down, unplugging, and being in the moment is a treat that I *want* to savor. Caring situates me in the world. It grounds me. Where the digital has a tenuous relationship with place and time, the analog is always in the here and the now. What sets caring for analog goods apart from caring for plants is that such care is usually folded into our other activities. We care for our records *as* we handle them, prepare them for play, and put them away. Our care for games is evident in our mindful handling of cards, in our awareness of environmental dangers (like drinks and sticky snacks), in carefully bagging up the various game components as we put them away. Our care for our books (or lack of it) is perhaps most evident in how we mark our spot when we pause our reading: with a bookmark, a dogeared corner, or simply cracking the spine as we put the book face-down on the ground. Care activities are *ongoing* activities, and as the analog is folded into the fabric of our lives, so too is care.

Self-care is often highlighted as a necessary concomitant of caregiving.* Caregiver burnout is a serious risk, whether you're a professional caregiver, caring for an aging parent, or simply a

*It's pretty ubiquitous advice, offered, for instance, by the National Institutes of Health: "[T]aking care of yourself isn't selfish; it's necessary for your health and well-being, which directly benefits the person you're caring for." ("Caring for Yourself while Caring for Others"). Yuriko Saito says it, too: "[I]f we neglect care for ourselves we cannot care for others" (*Aesthetics of Care*, 70).

parent yourself. I want to say more than this. I want to say that caring for others *is* self-care. That is, caring for others (whether people, pets, or things) is what makes someone *a caring being*. And caring, as I have suggested, *is a virtue*: a good state of character, a *quality* of persons. Insofar as we recognize caring as a virtue, we value *caring*, and not merely the people or things that we *care about*. And we care *that others care*—that, too, is something to be valued. Someone who embodies virtue is *doing it right*. For Aristotle, the virtues are necessary ingredients in *eudaimonia*, or human flourishing. Caring adds richness to life, and caring relationships provide an engaged and ongoing sense of purpose and connection with the world. Caring relationships have a way of grounding us—of making us present in our own lives—and that's true whether you're caring for a spouse, a plant, or a book. To me, that sounds like flourishing.*

Notes

1 See, e.g., Joseph L. Sax (1999), *Playing Darts with a Rembrandt: Public and Private Rights in Cultural Treasures* (Ann Arbor, MI: University of Michigan Press).

2 Yuriko Saito (2022), *Aesthetics of Care: Practice in Everyday Life* (London: Bloomsbury), 147.

3 Heritage Auctions, 'Heritage Auctions Celebrates World's First $28+ Million Comics Auction', *Heritage Auctions*, 8 April 2024,

---

*Not all virtue theorists are eudaimonists, and Aristotle in particular would have issues with grounding human flourishing in the material world.

https://comics.ha.com/heritage-auctions-press-releases-and-news/heritage-auctions-celebrates-world-s-first-28-million-comics-auction.s?releaseId=4945 (accessed 7 March 2025).

4 Aristotle (1980), *Nicomachean Ethics*, trans. David Ross (Oxford: Oxford University Press), 1157b29–1157b30; see Howard J. Curzer (2007), 'Aristotle: Founder of the Ethics of Care', *Journal of Value Inquiry* 41, 221–243.

5 Aristotle, *Nicomachean Ethics*, Book II: 1105a–1105b.

6 Nel Noddings (1984), *Caring: A Feminine Approach to Ethics & Moral Education* (Berkeley, CA: University of California Press), 148

7 Ibid., 149.

8 Ibid., 160.

9 Ibid., 162.

10 See Annette C. Baier (1995), *Moral Prejudices: Essays on Ethics* (Harvard University Press), 30–31.

11 See also Saito, *Aesthetics of Care*, 5.

12 Shaftesbury [Sir Anthony Ashley Cooper] (1999), *The Moralists*, in *Characteristics of Men, Manners, Opinions, Times*, 231–338 (University of Cambridge Press), III.2.

13 Immanuel Kant (1987), *Critique of Judgment*, trans. Werner S. Pluhar (Indianapolis: Hackett), §5.

14 John Dewey (1958), *Art as Experience* (New York: Capricorn Books), 11.

15 Sherri Irvin (2008), 'The Pervasiveness of the Aesthetic in Ordinary Experience', *British Journal of Aesthetics* 48(1), 29–44, at 30.

16 Irvin, 'The Pervasiveness of the Aesthetic,' 35.

17 See Tom Leddy, 'The Aesthetics of Washing Dishes', *Aesthetics Today*, 4 May 2018, https://aestheticstoday.blogspot.com/2018/05/the-aesthetics-of-washing-dishes.html (accessed 7 March 2025).

18 Robert M. Pirsig (1999), *Zen and the Art of Motorcycle Maintenance: An Inquiry into Values* (New York: William Morrow & Co.), 296.

19 Saito, *Aesthetics of Care*, 90.

20 Michelle Caswell and Marika Cifor (2016), 'From Human Rights to Feminist Ethics: Radical Empathy in the Archives', *Archivaria* 81, 23–43, at 31.

21 Leo Babauta, 'Mindful Simplicity: Decluttering, Cleaning & Leaving No Trace', *Zen Habits*, 4 September 2012, https://zenhabits.net/mindful-simplicity/ (accessed 7 March 2025).

22 John P. Miller (2019), *The Holistic Curriculum*, Third Edition (University of Toronto Press), 125.

23 Min-sun Lee, Juyoung Lee, Bum-Jin Park, and Yoshifumi Miyazaki (2015), 'Interaction with Indoor Plants May Reduce Psychological and Physiological Stress by Suppressing Autonomic Nervous System Activity in Young Adults: A Randomized Crossover Study', *Journal of Physiological Anthropology* 34(21). DOI 10.1186/s40101-014-0060-8.

24 Ahman Hassan, Chen Qibing, Jiang Tao, Lv Bing-Yang, Li Nian, Shu Li, Li Yu Tng, Ju Zhuo Li, Shang Guan Ziyue, and Muhammad Sohaib Tahir (2018), 'Effects of Plant Activity on Mental Stress in Young Adults', *HortScience* 53(1), 104–109.

25 Ellen J. Langer and Judith Rodin (1976), 'The Effects of Choice and Enhanced Personal Responsibility for the Aged: A Field Experiment in an Institutional Setting', *Journal of Personality and Social Psychology* 34(2), 191–198.

26 Judith Rodin and Ellen J. Langer (1977), 'Long-Term Effects of a Control-Relevant Intervention with the Institutionalized Aged', *Journal of Personality and Social Psychology* 35(12), 897–902.

27 Nardi Malis, Karina Fischer, Bess Dawson-Hughes, Endel J. Orav, Otto W. Meyer, Ursina Meyer, Sacha Beck, Hans-Peter Simmen, Hans-Christoph Pape, Andreas Egli, Walter C. Willett, Robert Theiler, and Heike A. Bischoff-Ferrari (2018), 'Association between Caregiver Role and Short- and Longer-Term Functional Recovery after Hip Fracture: A Prospective Study', *JAMDA* 19, 122–129, at 127.

Banana Ball
JESSE COLE
Banana Ball JESSE COLE

4

The Value of Agency

Power and Loss

I have just gotten off the phone with AT&T. Our Internet is down again. Upload and download speeds are both good, but there is just a trickle of data actually getting through. I can't stream anything on the TV, and most websites won't load on my phone. The technician runs a remote diagnostic that says everything is working fine, despite everything decidedly not working fine. After an hour of troubleshooting, the technician and I essentially shrug our shoulders and agree that we've run out of options. There's simply nothing I can do. I hang up. After an hour on the phone late in the afternoon, my phone is dying, so I plug it into the wall, pick up the book I started last night, and settle in with a glass of wine. I try to forget about my frustration with AT&T. After a couple more chapters in the book, I decide it isn't for me. Delaina suggests that I sell the book to our local used bookstore for some store credit. I certainly shop there enough that credit wouldn't be wasted. But I decide instead to put it in the Free

Little Library* at our local community garden—someone else might like to find this, and I can just walk it over.

That's something I can *do*. The digital realm, by contrast, tends to throw up barriers to *doing* such things.

I can't sell a digital book that I've purchased. I can't even give it away without giving away the device I read it on. In 2009, Barnes & Noble introduced the NOOK device, a competitor to Amazon's wildly popular Kindle. One feature of the NOOK that set it apart was the "LendMe" feature, which allowed users to lend the ebooks they had purchased to friends and family with NOOK devices or the NOOK app. In 2010, Amazon launched its own version of the feature, "Lending for Kindle." Each platform allowed you to lend an ebook to a friend for two weeks, during which time you (the owner of the ebook) would be unable to access it. There were some caveats, however. Whether an ebook could be "lent" on either platform was at the discretion of the publisher, and an ebook could only be "lent" once. It's important to be clear about this: it's not that you could only lend it to one friend at a time, or only to any given friend only once. Rather, once you have lent it once, to anyone, you never get to lend it *to anyone* ever again.[1] Amazon quietly discontinued the "Lending for Kindle" feature in 2023. Barnes & Noble, of course, can do the same at any time to "LendMe."

The central issue is that you haven't *really* purchased a copy of the ebook; you have purchased a digital license to *use* the ebook, and that license comes with limitations, some of them

---

*Freelittlelibrary.org

surprising.* In 2023, Kindle users found that their copies of books by Agatha Christie, Roald Dahl, and R.L. Stine had been altered overnight, either updated or edited to remove objectionable content. Part of that licensing agreement that users agree to—usually without reading it—allows Amazon to irrevocably alter the ebooks in your library without notifying you. It's not just ebooks, and it's not just Amazon. Both Google Play and Apple's terms and conditions note that media that you have "purchased"—ebooks, movies, music, video games—may be removed from its servers or from your own device at the company's discretion.[2]

When Hurricane Helene hit Greenville in 2024, it knocked out our power for a couple of days. We got lucky; others lost power for a week or more. We were all at the mercy of the technicians who had to go block-by-block through the city to restore power. I got a lot of reading done. We played a lot of games.

If the Internet goes out, I lose access to anything that isn't stored on my devices, and there's really not a lot I can do about it. The AT&T hub might give me an error code, but this is really only useful for the technician. When my printer runs into problems—which every printer does—it doesn't even give an error code; it just flashes an exclamation point at me. Of course, I have apps on my phone for all of this—an AT&T app for my Internet, a HP app for my printer, a separate app for my Internet

*You may want to add scare quotes around every instance of "purchased" and "owner" in the preceding paragraph… something you get to do with an analog copy.

signal extender, even an app for my thermostat—but these tend to be as opaque as the devices they connect with: perhaps I'll get an error code when something goes wrong; more than likely, it will just tell me that something *has* gone wrong. I'm tech-savvy enough to have figured that out on my own. I'm at the mercy of whatever technician I happen to get on the phone.

Digital technology tends to be frustrating because when things go wrong, there's usually simply not a lot you can do about it. In the British sitcom, *The IT Crowd*, the question "Have you tried turning it off and on again?" became a running joke, the first question asked of anyone upstairs who calls down for tech support. At one point, Roy—who usually answers the phone—has set up (ironically?) a reel-to-reel device to automatically ask that question upon taking any incoming call. When I called AT&T, it's the first thing I was asked, too: "Have you tried turning it off and on again?" And of course I had—and not just because "turning it off and on again" really *does* tend to solve the typical glitches, lags, and freezes that occasionally impede both digital work and play (Roy's recording offers no options for follow-up questions), but because it's really the only thing that the average user (even a self-proclaimed "tech-savvy" one like me) can do.

Digital licenses, opaque technology, and even reliance on the power grid limit my agency in appreciable ways, though we usually only notice this when things go wrong. When I come to think of technology as unreliable, I am going to experience a diminished sense of agency when I actually use it. We care about agency, and analog does a lot to put agency back in our own hands.[3]

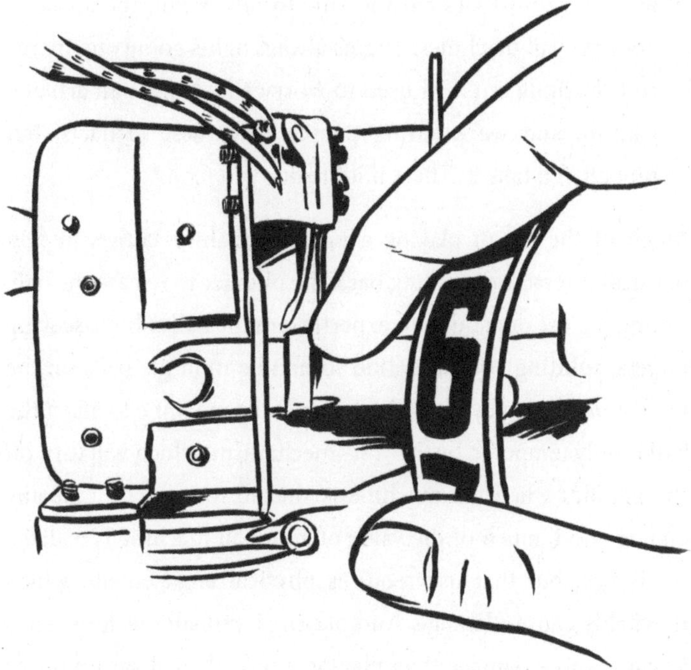

Getting Your Hands Dirty

Michael Schiess lifts the playfield from a 1990 *Back to the Future* pinball machine—the part of the machine with all the bumpers and paddles—and examines the underside. He replaces a lightbulb. There's *always* a lightbulb to replace. For Schiess, founder of the Pacific Pinball Museum, with its 90 working games, maintenance is a treadmill:

> You are literally beating the crap out of them every time you play a game. People, y'know, shove 'em around, I mean, people

> will *kick* 'em—that's hard for me to talk about, the abuse of poor pinball machines. There's always lights going out, there's coils burning out . . . I used to worry about it. It's an artifact, y'know, and we're letting people play these artifacts, but pinball, it'll take it. Then, if it breaks, you *fix* it.[4]

Much of the joy of playing a pinball machine comes in that physical interaction: pulling back the plunger to release the ball, timing the use of paddles to expertly aim the ball at high-scoring targets, splitting your attention to handle multiple balls on the field at once.* A player's desire to rattle the machine to affect the ball is only tempered by the "tilt" mechanism, which will turn off the paddles when the machine is shaken too much.† Like any analog good, much of the value of a pinball machine is realized in its use, but that use requires physical engagement, which inevitably causes damage. And playing a pinball machine tends to cause more damage than playing a record or playing a board game—but it's the sort of damage that *can* be repaired. Still, not just anybody can repair a pinball machine. "Nobody sells a working pinball machine," says Clay Harrell, who (among other things) writes pinball repair manuals. "If it was working, they wouldn't sell it. If you buy one, it's always broken."[5] Harrell is self-taught. At this point, pretty much every pinball repairman is—there's no school of pinball repair.

---

*Sega's 1995 *Apollo 13* game, tied in with the Ron Howard film of the same year, has a 13-ball multiball mode.

†The tilt mechanism consists of a metal ball hanging from a pendulum inside the console. If the machine is shaken too much, the ball will make contact with a ring surrounding it, setting off a tilt warning. Several such warnings will shut down gameplay.

Pinball machines are very big, very expensive, and require regular maintenance. Unlike video game cartridges—or even consoles—they are not easily or cheaply replaced. On Jacques Ellul's efficiency principle, they should be long gone, but they refuse to die. Indeed, like other forms of analog media, pinball is seeing a resurgence. However, for those looking to maintain and repair their machines, there is no easy onramp. In part because each machine is so specific, there is no sufficiently broad book of pinball machine repair to cover every issue that might arise. Instead, analog enthusiasts will turn to the web, either to YouTube videos or to the crowdsourced PinWiki.com, an expansive compendium of pinball maintenance and repair. And they are doing so in ever-growing numbers.* The hands-on nature of the game isn't a deterrent. People like playing pinball, and they don't mind getting their hands dirty.

In *Technology and the Character of Contemporary Life*, Albert Borgmann notes that technological development continually moves towards requiring less of us, of moving to the background: "The machinery makes no demands on our skill, strength, or attention, and it is less demanding the less it makes its presence felt."[6] That is, until it stops working. After my frustrating encounter with the AT&T technician, Delaina tried calling back later in the day, hoping she might get to talk to a more helpful person. She did, indeed, and the new technician found the fix.

---

*A YouTube video, "Repairing Bally's WIZARD Pinball Machine – Strange Motor Problem," posted by Joe's Classic Video Games in May of 2024 has garnered more than 11,000 views in eight months.

Apparently our Internet hub needed updates, and had to be reset to factory settings to get them. We can reset our hub to factory settings by holding down the reset button for 10 seconds, but the technician recommended that we don't do so without calling AT&T first, so that they can monitor our device remotely while we reset it. If we try to fix it on our own, she said, we could cause more problems. The joy that I had felt in having the Internet problem fixed was thus quickly muffled: when it happens again—and it will—there's nothing that *I* can do about it. I'm confident that I *could* learn to fix a pinball machine (if I could afford one in the first place), but there's not a lot I can do for my AT&T hub when it fritzes—AT&T has taken that out of my hands.

There is a distinct value to a thing that I can understand, a thing that I can fix, and this will always be part of the appeal of analog. Technology—particularly *digital* technology—aims at eliminating the user's involvement with that technology: press, play, and forget about it. We simply don't notice it when practices and technology become entrenched in our lives because they move to the background. Analog tends to fall outside this pattern, because it tends to require—and it responds to—our attention, and so it actively *engages* us. The return to analog is, in part, a reembracing of the understanding of the *means* and the appeal of getting your hands dirty.

There is certainly an appeal to the Tesla, with all of its driver-assistance systems and automatic software updates. But the clean appeal of the Tesla will always be mirrored by the dirty appeal of the hotrod, which requires hands-on attention and embodies agency.* It isn't just repair. It's just that repair is a special kind of doing, and the *doing* is the thing. We see the same sort of dirty appeal in fixing a radio, in gardening, in making espresso, in crafting. Each of these hands-on activities requires slowing down and working through a process. Working with analog feels *inefficient*, and that's kind of the point. Slowing down puts you *in* the process. Slowing down is a good way to feel agency.

---

*Once, when I was a teenager, my father was telling me a story about doing maintenance on his car when *he* was a teenager (so, sometime in the 1950s), and he got to the part of the story where he was fixing the car's battery. I stopped him mid-sentence: "What do you mean, you were *fixing the battery*?" He explained that, back in the day, you could open up a car battery, test the electrolyte levels, and top off the cells with distilled water when necessary. You can't really do that anymore. Most car batteries today are "sealed" or "maintenance free," designed to be thrown out when they've run their course, rather than repaired. The average car owner can do some *light* maintenance on a battery—mostly cleaning up corrosion that builds up on the battery terminals—and that's about it. When the battery goes (and it will), you had better have a friend you can call for a jump so you can get it to Manny, Moe, and Jack (or whoever runs your local auto parts store). Indeed, that's fairly indicative of what today's average car owner can do to maintain their vehicle as a whole: keep an eye on the tires and fluids, and take it to a professional when things go wrong. Once upon a time, the average teenager could (in principle) learn how to maintain their entire car, down to stripping and rebuilding an engine—to fix their car with their own hands. The digitization of automotive technology has literally taken most auto repair out of the average person's hands. As my friend Angela puts it, "What a thing to have lost." Where "auto shop" was once a standard high-school course offering, these are fewer and further between, and limited in their scope. Your average neighborhood mechanic isn't going to be able to repair the electronic control unit that controls most of the systems in a modern car, but at best replace it when it goes haywire. Automotive manufacturers began incorporating digital technology into cars to improve efficiency and performance, but such efficiency will always have a cost in sense of agency.

Embracing Agency

There is a growing subgenre of stories (in novels, film, comics, television) that I would broadly describe as *cozy post-apocalyptic*: the world as we know it has collapsed—whether through war, natural disaster, or disease—and the survivors work to get by without modern conveniences. The apocalypse itself is within living memory, and we follow a group as they acclimate to their new world. Invariably, that world has become distinctly regional, and people's lives are largely defined by their place in their communities, finding their new niche. What sets the cozy post-apocalypse apart from the much larger category of post-apocalypse literature is that the survivors are generally *enjoying* their new world. They struggle, yes, but they find fulfillment in the simpler lifestyle that the world provides. Imagine *Little House on the Prairie*, but in the future, *after* the electronics are gone, or the zombie apocalypse minus the zombies.* Back to basics. Recent years have seen several books emerge in this subgenre, including Emily St. John Mandel's *Station Eleven* and (perhaps most notably) James Howard Kunstler's *World Made by Hand* series.† In *A History of the Future*—the second book in Kunstler's

*In this way, the cozy post-apocalypse has a healthy overlap with stories that fall into the "modern Robinsonade," modeled on Daniel Defoe's classic survival-adventure story.

†Ironically, there are even video games in the cozy post-apocalyptic subgenre, like *Among Trees*, where players must fish for their food, craft their own tools, and improve their broken-down cabin in the woods. An earlier cozy post-apocalyptic book is Kim Stanley Robinson's *The Wild Shore*, first in the *Three Californias* series.

series—Andrew, formerly an editor of scientific books and journals, finds himself the new librarian of Union Grove, New York (having dusted off the old card catalogs), a portrait painter (now the only method for recording likenesses), and a part-time repairer of old mechanical clocks (much in demand without electricity to rely on). Andrew is very much the Analog Man. Andrew lives in a Gothic cottage he has largely restored himself, making his own house paint from linseed oil, turpentine, and foraged pigment. Andrew, like many of those in Union Grove, is *thriving*: "The world," Kunstler writes, "was singing in all his cells."[7]

In the inaugural 2014 Ipsos Global Trends study, surveying more than 16,000 participants in 20 countries, six in ten reported "constantly looking at screens these days," the same proportion that reported craving a simpler life.[8] And those numbers seem to be trending upwards.[9] Against this backdrop, the rise of cozy post-apocalyptic stories is not surprising; the genre represents, I think, a broader yearning to be more involved in our own lives, a yearning that is expressed in the explosion of sourdough baking during the pandemic, the growing homesteader movement, and the story of the Luddite Club, a group of Brooklyn students first profiled in the *New York Times* in 2022.[10] The club was founded by teenager Logan Lane, who traded in her smartphone for a flip phone during the COVID-19 lockdown. Technology, she realized, had finally invaded every part of her life.*

*It wasn't just Lane.

> My phone kept the curated lives of my peers with me wherever I went, following me to the dinner table, to the bus stop, and finally to my bed where I fell asleep groggy and irritable, often at late hours in the night, clutching my device.[11]

It was addictive, it was draining, and it was looking inescapable:

> I think when I started to realize that the pandemic was going to be a longer thing than I had initially expected, I would see other people doing reading challenges or knitting, just using the extra time for some artistic activity. And I felt like I was the type of person who ought to be doing that, but I wasn't. I was wasting it on TikTok or Instagram. I felt for myself, if I was going to be productive, I needed to take a step back from the phone.[12]

Lane took the plunge, powered down her smartphone, and stuffed it in a drawer in her parents' room. She began borrowing books from the Brooklyn Public Library, stepping out to read them next door on a bench in Prospect Park. She took up sewing. She acquired a typewriter and a cassette player. The next year, after returning to in-person classes at Edward R. Murrow High School, Lane met another student with a flip phone, Jameson Butler, and the Luddite Club was founded. Soon, there were a dozen or more members coming out on Sunday afternoons to meet in person in Prospect Park. "Luddites are frequently late," Lane reports, "which personally is a pet peeve of mine."[13] The price of inefficiency. Part book club, part knitting circle, part art collective, the Luddite Club invited other teens to come out and put their phones away, too. One by one, the regulars traded their smartphones for flip phones. As one founding member puts it, the best thing about a flip phone is snapping it shut.[14]

Ironically, that *Times* article by Alex Vadukul went viral. Hundreds of people emailed Vadukul, trying to reach the students who had put themselves out of reach of digital technology.[15] Hardly a news outlet failed to profile the Luddite Club. Political activist and perennial Presidential candidate Ralph Nader praised the club in an op-ed.[16] Like a scene out of *Fight Club*, new Luddite Clubs started popping up around the world. The kids had tapped into something.

Two years later, now in college, Lane landed an internship with Light Phone, which manufactures a minimalist cell phone that only allows for texting and calling.[17] She continues to be the face of the modern Luddite movement, giving talks at that same Brooklyn Library, and at the Museum of Modern Art. Other founding members, like Lola Shub, found they couldn't navigate college without a smartphone:

> It's the relief of knowing I can do things easier. . . . I feel like I'm not trying as hard anymore. When I had the flip phone, I had to put in effort to get to places, to talk to people. Everything was a task. Now it's easy to do things. I guess I still don't like needing the crutch of a smartphone, though I couldn't figure out how to go on without one.

Lane is hopeful that she can stay the course:

> I have my flip phone because I still need to have one, whether that's for school or staying connected with my parents. But I

> think the dream for me is to be unreachable one day. To have no phone at all.

The appeal of analog does not represent for most people (certainly not for me) a desire to return to nature (à la Rousseau), nor a desire "to be unreachable," but rather a return to a richer engagement with the everyday, a deeper involvement in daily activities, and by extension, a slower life.

Agency and Balance

Technology has an interesting relationship with agency. There can be a *lot* of struggling with analog—a lot of finagling. Analog photography proves to be an especially good example. As digital photography took off, the business of analog photography suffered accordingly. For over a century the leader in film photography, Kodak filed for Chapter 11 bankruptcy protection in 2012. If what you wanted was to capture a moment, pretty much everybody already carried a digital camera with them at all times, which never needed film, which always auto-focused, which was not restricted in the number of images it could capture, and which didn't require paying and waiting a week to get photos back from a kiosk in a mall parking lot (only to find out you had your thumb over the lens, or the flash didn't go off). But, like all of the other forms of analog media we have talked about, film photography refused to die. A year after Kodak filed for bankruptcy, it reemerged. Its much-dwindled film business had been handed to a new spin-off company, Kodak Alaris, owned by the original company's creditors, which responded to a small but steadily growing demand, reviving film products that had been discontinued years earlier. And, as other film companies shuttered their doors, analog enthusiasts swept in to claim their equipment. But they faced a steep learning curve.

The chemicals used to make, treat, and develop analog film are notoriously fickle. Back when I was my high school's yearbook editor, I somehow managed to ruin several rolls of film in the development process. I have no idea how. Since much of this process has to be performed in pitch darkness, I don't know if I mixed two chemicals that shouldn't be mixed, if I simply used the wrong chemical, if I somehow diluted the developing fluid, or if some light somehow managed to sneak in. I am gladdened to learn that this is pretty indicative of the perils of film generally. Mirko Böddecker, CEO of Adox Film, a small German company whose history largely parallels Kodak's, addresses the challenges of reviving analog film in a 2019 keynote address:

> Even up to today, what we're doing here—manufacturing film—is still to a certain extent a black box. This means there have been thousands, if not tens of thousands, of highly-skilled scientists working for decades to find out how to make a good film, how to make these grains which are light-sensitive and which eventually form the image. But nobody can observe it, because they're sensitive to light. . . . So nobody can see what's going on when we make such a film. And, since 150 years, it's still trial-and-error. It's very complex interactions of

> all the chemicals. We put up to 150 chemicals in the film. If it's color film, it's even more. Even small impurities can ruin entire film batches.[18]

Böddecker goes on to relay a story told to him by one of the technicians who had come to Adox from Agfa, another casualty of the decline of analog film in the early 2000s.

> They constantly had failures in production of Agfa film, and they didn't know what was the reason. And after two or three months, they finally found out that one of the guys stirring the kettle had changed his deodorant. And this was enough to ruin 1000 liters of emulsion.

This, of course, makes me feel a little better about screwing up whatever it was I screwed up in my high school darkroom. But I have no desire to return to the darkroom. I am perfectly happy with the agency that my iPhone affords me. The level of agency that film photography offered was more than I was looking for. Nearly every form of analog requires users to choose their level of agency.

Just a little north of me, in Asheville, North Carolina, there is a museum dedicated to Robert Moog, the inventor of the first commercial analog synthesizer, the Moog. Delaina and I took a tour of the small museum, and marveled at the interactive displays, but we had little understanding of what we were looking at. Each Moog synthesizer has a keyboard, yes, but this is overshadowed by an enormous modular board of switches, dials, and sockets, all connected by a tangle of patch chords,

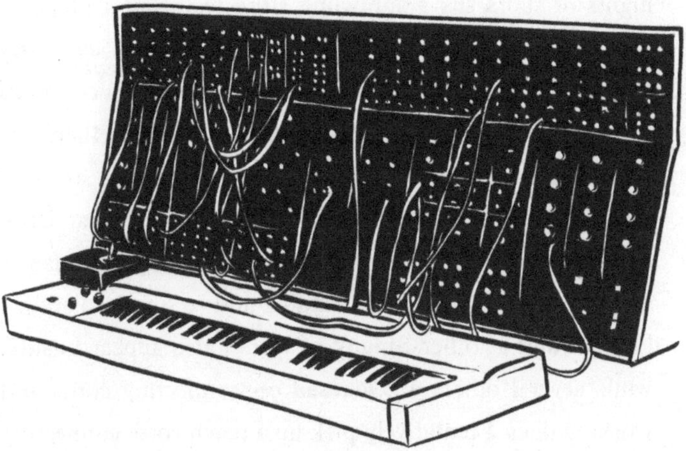

allowing the keyboardist to employ oscillators, noise generators, amplifiers, filters, modulators, and all manner of other tools to shape sound. And it is all analog—all hands-on. A few years after Delaina and I had marveled at these towers of wonder, we invited our friends Pete and Maria, who were down from Pennsylvania, to come back to the Moogseum with us. Our friends are musicians, and they spent another hour at the tiny museum after Delaina and I had finished our tour and went to find coffee. What was baffling to us was engrossing to them.

In a 2024 study, Michael Beverland, Karen Fernandez, and Giana Eckhardt set out to explore how the resurgence of analog intersected with feelings of agency. Beverland set out to purchase an analog synthesizer, his first foray into that domain:

> I finally locate the legendary Schneiders Buero, a store for analog synthesizers in Berlin's "Kotti" neighborhood. Up two

> flights of stairs sits a sprawling store featuring a range of modular analog synths, including names such as Moog and Buchla, as well as modern Euro-racks. Each setup contains headphones and boxes of patch cables. There are no instructions and the machines, while alluring, are also somewhat imposing. Like others, I choose a modular setup and glance over the knobs and switches, looking at the labels signaling wave form, pitch, volume and so on. Perplexed, I look around at others, many of whom also appear unsure, while several others are focused on connecting cords and working dials. I tentatively pick up a patch cord, connecting two modules. Nothing. I keep going, and eventually sounds emerge. After a while I realize I've been at this for two hours. Somewhat dazed, I look around, many of those who began using the machines at the same time as me are locked in thought while moving to their music, their machines covered in patch cords.[19]

There are no shortcuts to using an analog synthesizer: absolutely everything is adjusted manually. At first, I typed "everything *has to* be adjusted manually." Either may be right, depending on what you're looking for. If you have a sense of what to do with all of these switches, dials, and patch cords, I am certain it is an enlivening proposition, a chance to play, to feel agency. But if you're at the base of that learning curve, it will be daunting, a *burden* of agency. The more that technology is automated, the less of a sense of agency users tend to feel in engaging with that technology.[20] On the other hand, that same sense of agency can quickly be overwhelmed by all of the choices available to the user.* Beverland, Fernandez, and Eckhardt note that novices with some particular analog form (say, standing before a Moog synthesizer) feel an "almost unlimited range of choice," and this may itself produce a feeling of a lack of control.[21] A sense of control requires at least some mastery and understanding of a form's inherent limitations. The learning curve with some analog technology can be a serious barrier to entry for the analog-curious.

Like the Luddite Club, stepping back from a digital world that is the only world they have known, like the wave of young vinyl enthusiasts buying their first turntables so they can play the latest Beyoncé album, the renewed interest in both film photography and analog synthesizers is being led by the next generations, who are looking for something that the digital doesn't offer—something antithetical to its nature. Embracing analog is taking a stand against the increasing tide of ease and unencumbrance promised by the digital—of tasks being taken out of our hands. To many, this will seem like an odd stand to make, and an odd place to make it. Certainly, the Luddites had their critics and detractors. After all, why stand *against* ease? Why stand *for* encumbrance? And if struggle is what we want, why not make things *really* hard on ourselves? Why not eschew *all* such modern conveniences? Why not live like the Amish? Why not build a cabin on Walden Pond? Why not just live in a cave? For the younger generations who make up a plurality of analog enthusiasts, who grew up in a digital world, the embrace

---

*In his 2004 bestseller, Barry Schwartz calls this "the paradox of choice."

of analog is not a *return to anything*, but is a *new* adventure, a power to choose the level of inconvenience they want, or need, to bring them the engagement they desire from their daily activities. And each of us has to choose that on our own.

Last chapter, we talked about the attempt that Delaina and I made to buy a vintage turntable. After that debacle, Delaina begrudgingly accepted that a vintage record changer might be the wrong choice for us, so we started researching the surprisingly complicated world of modern turntables. What we quickly learned is that the higher-end the machine, the more work it is. Lower-end machines have automatic everything, and have nothing to adjust. Turntables aimed at audiophiles exchange convenience for fine control. The higher up you go, the more adjustments you can (and have to) make, including manually adjusting the belt as you change from playing LPs to 45s, adjusting the length, height, and angle of the tonearm, and adjusting the amount of force that the needle puts on the record.* We settled on something at the lower end of the higher end: no automatic return on the arm at the end of the record, but no weights or belts to adjust.

Craft and Agency

For a few years in the mid-2010s, adult coloring books experienced a surprising sales boom, a surge that experts largely

---

*Of course, even with a high-end turntable and properly balanced tonearm, the needle is slowly, slowly degrading the vinyl.

trace back to Johanna Basford's 2013 bestseller, *Secret Garden: An Inky Treasure Hunt and Coloring Book for Adults.* Basford's line-drawing is clean and whimsical, varying from the simple to the complex—sometimes strikingly design-forward, drawing on Basford's background in label design, and sometimes looking like wandering organic doodles. In 2015, *Secret Garden*, and Basford's follow-up, *Enchanted Forest*, were the two bestselling books on Amazon.[22] That same year, Michael O'Mara Books, which introduced its line of adult coloring books a few years earlier, reported, "We've never seen a phenomenon like it in our thirty years of publishing. We are on our fifteenth reprint of some of our titles. Just can't keep them in print fast enough."[23] By 2023, Basford reports, she had sold 25 million coloring books, all aimed at adults.[24] Sales of colored pencils spiked by nearly 50% in 2015.[25]

Coloring is time away from the screen—a little respite at the end of your day that isn't about getting something done, that isn't focused on most efficiently accomplishing a goal, that isn't being done for someone else. And, rather than mindlessly scrolling through listicles and TikTok videos, you are *concentrating*, putting *yourself* into something. Coloring is process-oriented, it is hands-on, and it is immersive. Nothing happens without you doing it. Author and blogger Amanda Diehl writes, "There's something unique about spending hours coloring individual sections, your face obnoxiously close to the paper as you sit hunched over your coffee table, and then pulling back to look at the entirety of your work."[26] Psychologist Scott Barry Kaufman suggests that coloring "can provide people with a way to flex their creativity."[27] And getting that taste of creativity seemed to help many realize what was missing in their day-to-day lives.* Coloring is *craft*, and craft embodies *agency*.

As an object of philosophical inquiry, craft was largely kicked to the side in the modern era as philosophers were carving the new category of *art* out of the older, broader category of *technê*. *Technê*, a Greek word, once described everything from portraiture to bricklaying to weaving—anything that fell under the understanding of skillful making. But in the eighteenth and nineteenth centuries, philosophers came to treat *art* as essentially intellectual; what remained of that older category was the essentially sensual and material: *craft*. Artists, it was understood, worked first with their *minds*; craftspeople—artisans—worked first with their hands. The craftsperson followed a rule; the artist created *new* rules. *Artists* created sculptures, sonatas, and poetry; *artisans* made cabinets, pottery, and quilts. Craft took skill, yes, but artists had something more: Kant called it *genius*, a quality had by artists but not mere artisans.† This philosophical turn to

*In a 2015 *New Yorker* article, Adrienne Raphael linked the popularity of adult coloring books to a "broader cultural shift" towards regressive activities, like adult summer camp. There is something to this. With lives that are increasingly dictated for them, I expect, children too would relish the little bit of agency that coloring books provide. The popularity of the hobby produced a wave of journalism looking to explain the boom. Many suggest that the activity of coloring is simply relaxing. Some go further to suggest it is meditative, which would certainly align with my thoughts from last chapter. Others have gone so far as to suggest that adult coloring books can be therapeutic, a claim that therapists have tended to push back on.

†Women (it was understood) generally lacked genius, and so were largely excluded from the *arts*, and relegated to craftwork, working with textiles and (at best) clay. Art school doors were closed to them.

the intellectual set up a longstanding conceptual rift between *art* and *craft*. Meanwhile, the emergence of automated production around the same time created a third category of object: *products*—the result of neither art nor craft.*

That new distinction between art, craft, and product is perhaps nowhere better embodied than in Marcel Duchamp's "ready-made" sculpture, *Fountain*, an otherwise ordinary porcelain urinal signed with a pseudonym—*R. Mutt*—and famously submitted to the inaugural exhibition of the Society of Independent Artists in 1917. Duchamp took a *product*, the output of technology, and using *no craft whatsoever*, but only his own genius, transfigured that product into *art*. To many at the time, and to many today, *Fountain* sounds like some kind of joke—a bit of toilet humor, as it were. But a 2004 survey of British art experts voted *Fountain* the single most influential work in the history of modern art. Certainly, it signaled a sort of sea change.

From Duchamp, we get Dada, we get installation art, and we get *conceptual art*—a category that places primary value on the *idea behind* the art, rather than on the finished product or the process of getting there. Sol LeWitt sketched out the idea:

> In conceptual art the idea or concept is the most important aspect of the work. When an artist uses a conceptual form of art, it means that all of the planning and decisions are made

---

*Institutions of art—both art schools and museums—largely adopted these same distinctions. Larry Shiner thus suggests that "craft as a category has been *relational* from the beginning, positioned between industrial production on one side and fine art on the other" (Shiner, "Blurred Boundaries," 233).

> beforehand and the execution is a perfunctory affair. . . . It is usually free from the dependence on the skill of the artist as a craftsman. . . . What the work of art looks like isn't too important.[28]

If you walk into a showing of contemporary art, and you don't "get" it, that's Duchamp's influence.

Still, not everyone got on board. At the same time that Duchamp was exploding on the art scene, the celebrated Italian painter Giorgio de Chirico was warning artists that they were at risk of losing something critical, and rallied a return to craft, with all its hands-on slowness and struggle:

> To return to the craft! This will not be easy and will demand time and toil. [. . .] To return to the craft, our painters must be extremely diligent in the perfection of their means: canvas, colours, brushes, oils and varnishes must be of the highest quality. [. . .] It would be a good thing if painters again took up the habit of making their own canvas and colours. Rather more patience and effort is necessary: but, when the painter has understood once and for all that the execution of a painting is not a thing to be carried out in the shortest possible time, a thing merely to be exhibited or sold to a dealer; when he has understood that the same painting should be worked on for months, even years, until it is completely smooth and polished; and until the painter's conscience is completely clear; when he has understood this he will not find it difficult to sacrifice a few hours a day to the preparation of his own canvases and colours. He will do it with care and with love.[29]

Despite his decidedly intellectual leanings (being best known for his "metaphysical paintings," a sort of precursor to the surrealists, grounded in the philosophies of Arthur Schopenhauer and Friedrich Nietzsche), de Chirico believed that art was importantly material, sensual, and personal.

Certainly, there are artists, following Duchamp, who prefer not to involve themselves in the material making of art, some of them very famous. Anish Kapoor (best known for Chicago's giant metallic sculpture, *Cloud Gate*, affectionately known as "The Bean") and Jeff Koons (best known for his stainless-steel replicas of balloon dogs and inflatable rabbits) come to mind. Neither Kapoor nor Koons actually *makes* the objects he is known for. Rather, each leaves it to hired fabricators to bring their visions to life. But, at least in my experience, when members of the general public learn how Kapoor and Koons work, they tend to retract the label of "artist." My students similarly push back at the case of *Fountain*.

In his 1938 treatise, *Principles of Art*, philosopher R.G. Collingwood sought to make the art/craft distinction on the basis that craft is essentially ends-directed, while art is not. That is, the artisan has in mind some outcome—a cabinet, a blanket, a pair of socks—and uses their learned skills to achieve that end. The artist, by contrast, has no particular end in mind, and does not know where she is going until she gets there. The craftsperson is always chained to their end, while the artist is free to wander as their heart desires. Manufacturing would seem, then, to be a sort of purified, perfected craft on Collingwood's view—a perfect mechanization of means to end.

But, importantly, where manufacturing aims at mass standardization, craft is shaped by human hands. Even where a craftsperson is making another blanket, another mug, another cabinet, we *expect* to find variation—evidence of human agency in the making of *this thing*. Craft is very much in the *doing*—the molding, the selecting, the feel of the brush—all of which gets handwaved by Collingwood. Collingwood talks of craft as *imposing a plan on matter*,[30] and this is where I think he grossly misunderstands craft. Artisans often talk in terms of a *dialog* between themselves and their chosen materials, rather than imposing their will upon it.

Take pottery. The first step of pottery is centering the clay on the wheel—working with the lump of material to find a rotating symmetrical central axis before forming the lump into a pot. This sounds simple, but is notoriously challenging even for seasoned potters, and involves a sensitivity to the qualities of the

clay—textured or slick, firm or soft—that takes patience and years to master. Poet, potter, and co-founder of Black Mountain Press, M.C. Richards, describes the process:

> The bringing of the clay into a spinning, unwobbling pivot, which will then be free to take innumerable shapes as potter and clay press against each other. The firm, tender, sensitive pressure which yields as much as it asserts. It is like a hand clasp between two living hands, receiving the greeting at the very moment that they give it. It is this speech between the hand and the clay that makes me think of dialogue. And it is a language far more interesting than the spoken vocabulary which tries to describe it, for it is spoken, not by the tongue and lips, but by the whole body, by the whole person, speaking and listening.[31]

Archaeologist Lambros Malafouris describes the interaction between a potter and their clay as a *kinaesthetic transaction* or *haptic attentive unity*—as "the feeling of mindful presence characteristic of the state of attentive material engagement."[32] Many talk about this feeling in terms of what psychologist Mihály Csíkszentmihályi famously dubbed the *flow state*.

Artisans and scholars of craft often reject talk of "agency" as improperly suggesting a one-way causal relationship from maker to object. Rather, anthropologist Tim Ingold suggests that pottery "is not . . . an imposition of form on matter but a contraposition of equal and opposed forces immanent respectively in gesturing hands and wet clay."[33] The potter pushes, and the clay pushes back. Indeed, rather than rejecting talk of agency, I would suggest that it is precisely *in* this exchange with the material that we *feel* our own agency: we feel ourselves in the activity, our agency is embodied, we are immersed.* As I experience the clay, I experience myself.

Where artisans of all types speak of the value of process, of immersion of the self in practice, so much of digital creation seems invested in most efficiently reaching the end product. Cutting and pasting keeps me from having to recreate from scratch; macros allow me to trigger a series of tasks for the computer to perform, rather than having to perform every one of them myself, over and over, again and again. Indeed, we now live in an age where computer programs will offer to do my writing for me, to skip over all that struggle. In this way, generative artificial intelligence is the apotheosis of the digital, and the antithesis of craft. Image generators like Midjourney and Dall-E can create in seconds what it would take a skilled artist hours or days to create (after years of training and practice), all for a surprisingly low monthly subscription fee. Who needs craft when you have A.I.?

In part because the nature of this book has been exploratory rather than argument driven, each paragraph you have read so far has probably taken, on average, longer to write than any other paragraph I have written elsewhere of equivalent length. It has

---

*Ceramicist Harvey Littleton offers this: "Essential to the artist's work with glass is his understanding of the material and the basic, element subconscious action-reaction of man and material, not only in the forming of the hot glass – the melting and the forming – but in the complete integration of man and material in a totally controlled time-space concept" (*Glassblowing: A Search for Form*, 13).

been a struggle, and it has occurred to me on several occasions that I could probably have had ChatGPT write the book in a day. When I think of this book-in-progress as a *product*, the draw of A.I. is overwhelming. But then I remember that I'm not writing the book to have another book with my name on it. I remember why I set out to write it: as a reason to explore my own values. That's not something A.I. can do for me. And when I think of it as *craft*, as a *process*, I can enjoy the struggle of figuring out exactly what word to put here, exactly the best way to arrange my thoughts. It's when I feel most human.

If all that you want of art is a product, then A.I. is the tool for you. And if you are a working commercial artist—someone in the business of making art *products*—you can either adapt to A.I. or get out of the way. Certainly, the current state of A.I. produces struggles of its own. If I have some image or idea in mind, I must struggle to craft a prompt to get the algorithm to produce something close to what I envision, and that's often a long and frustrating process. Often, I try again and again without success, usually giving up and accepting something *close enough*. But this struggle is not a *feature* of working with A.I. Rather, like my struggle with AT&T, it is a bug. Indeed, there is a thriving industry in prompt engineering for those with neither the time nor inclination to struggle with fine-tuning their own wording. Perhaps by the time you read this, that problem will have been solved, and the prompt engineers, too, will be out of business.

Philosopher Anthony Cross suggests that, when it comes to working with generative A.I., "[w]hat is perhaps most striking about the process is its *ease*: it is possible to create hundreds of images quite quickly. This often facilitates a sort of playful exploration and generation."[34] I'm not suggesting it isn't *possible* to approach A.I. generation with an eye on process, facilitating play and the experience of agency, but rather that the *point* of the technology seems to be at odds with this approach. Cross writes, "AI contributes to a creative process guided by a human artist which is ultimately oriented towards the *production* of some artistic output."[35] It's that ends-oriented thinking that is the appeal of A.I., and if we could get A.I. to just skip right to what's in my mind, most users would be thrilled. But for artists, craft—the means—was a thing to be valued in itself. It was not a problem to be overcome, but one to be worked through. Exploring that wide-open landscape between idea and product is something that artists and artisans alike (insofar as there is any real distinction) *enjoy*. And wrestling with the material limitations of analog art is very much a feature for many of them. Sociologist and apprentice glassblower Erin O'Connor notes: "Proficient glassblowers have often said that glassblowing is not about blowing the perfect piece of glass, but coming up with effective solutions to all the problems that consistently present themselves in the process of glassblowing."[36] Craftspeople *take up* craft, not because they want the product that the craft produces—and which is much more cheaply and easily produced by other means—but because they want to be *involved* in the making. De Chirico spoke of creating with care and love, and care and love—like craft—are about a relationship with an individual.

Johanna Basford advises newcomers to adult coloring books: "Don't worry if you go over the lines! Colouring isn't about the pursuit of perfection. There are no rules. I want people to enjoy the creative process, relax, have fun, play a little."[37] Although seemingly clearly aimed at an end—a colored image—coloring-book enthusiasts tend (like others who craft) to focus instead on the process. Neuroscientist and avid coloring book enthusiast Jordan Gaines Lewis writes:

> When I color, I'm not actually accomplishing anything productive; I may spend several meticulous hours on a single picture before simply shoving the book back onto my shelf. And then what am I supposed to do with it — tape it up on my fridge? . . . But here's a wild thought: Not everything we do must be in pursuit of productivity.[38]

If you just wanted the image colored, there are certainly more efficient ways to do it. Scan the image into Photoshop, Canva, or Procreate—click, click, click, and you're done. If you're just looking to color *something*, an array of cheap coloring-book apps let you skip the analog step entirely. But there is a decided preference among coloring book enthusiasts for the analog version of the activity.

The Experience of Agency

In 1991, the Williams Manufacturing Company released the *Terminator II: Judgment Day* pinball game, launched to coincide with the release of the blockbuster James Cameron film. Instead of a manual spring plunger, the game used a stylized gun handle with trigger to launch the ball. Some future games adopted a similar feature, but replacing the stylized trigger with a simple button—the "autoplunger." Traditional spring-plungers were more expensive to produce and needed more maintenance than autoplungers, and autoplungers allowed for a range of new game features. *Terminator II*, for example, allowed the player to launch several balls in succession like an automatic weapon—something that spring plungers wouldn't allow for. Displays for pinball machines began incorporating digital animation around this same time. Pinball enthusiasts were used to bells and whistles, and digital displays added without taking away. But for many, replacing the traditional spring-plunger with a push button took something important away. Rare is the pinball enthusiast who prefers pushing a launch button to pulling a spring plunger. Where games with push-buttons are enjoyed, it is because the push-button launch allows for game *features* (like auto-fire) that a traditional spring plunger does not. Conversely, those who enjoy the spring plunger prefer it for the sense of control it provides—for the *feel* of it.

In his 2020 book, *Games: Agency as Art*, philosopher C. Thi Nguyen argues that what makes games special is how they create and manipulate agency:

> A game tells us to take up a particular goal. It designates abilities for us to use in pursuing that goal. It packages that all up with a set of obstacles, crafted to fit those goals and abilities. A game uses all these elements to sculpt a form of activity. And when we play games, we take on an alternate form of agency. We take on new goals and accept different sets of

abilities. We give ourselves over to different—and focused—ways of inhabiting our own agency.[39]

In most games, at least, players strive for some end that is built into the game's rules. The game's rules tell us what to care about. To play that game is to invoke a certain, temporary form of agency, to take on intentional action aimed at the prescribed end. Nguyen describes agency as "action for a reason,"[40] and the experience of that agency, Nguyen argues, has a decidedly aesthetic dimension.

Cognitive neuroscientists (including philosophers, psychologists, and others) use the term "sense of agency" to mean something like "sense of control," and standardly unpack the term in two ways, each with its own sort of test. First, a subject will *report* on their own experience, stating whether and to what degree they felt like they were in control of their actions. This sort of *explicit judgment of agency* is necessarily conscious, conceptual, and interpretive. Second, researchers will look to what they call an *implicit feeling of agency*, a sort of background experience, usually perceived only as a background coherent flow, and usually only noticed when it is interrupted. To test *this*, researchers have zeroed in on what is called "intentional binding," a feeling that time between intentional action and associated effect is compressed. Where explicit judgment of agency is a matter of self-awareness, implicit feeling of agency is pre-conceptual, a matter of background perceptual processing.[41]

Certainly, a sense of control is *part* of what I mean when I talk about the experience of agency. But I mean something more, too—what I can perhaps best describe as a feeling of being *actively involved* in my own activities, a feeling of being *embodied* and *present* in my own actions. It may be easiest to understand that feeling by looking at what it's like when it's missing.

It may come as no surprise that those whose lives became heavily screen-based during COVID-19 lockdowns—living out their days in Zoom meetings and social media, in front of the television, playing video games—reported increased symptoms of what psychologists call *depersonalization* and (more generally) *derealization*: a lack of connection to their own actions or to the world around them.[42] Reports of depersonalization and derealization indicate a lack of "presence" in the world. About 1–2% of people report feelings of depersonalization, but this is much higher among younger people. A little less than half of college students report having experienced feelings of depersonalization.[43] These reports peaked during the pandemic, right when we saw spikes in already-rising sales of analog goods, right when the Luddite Club formed. People—and young people especially—needed to feel grounded in their own worlds, to find an anchor to keep from floating away.

In his 2009 bestseller, *Shop Class as Soulcraft* (sort of a *Zen and the Art of Motorcycle Maintenance* 2.0), philosopher-turned-motorcycle-mechanic Matthew B. Crawford writes:

> Thinking about manual engagement seems to require nothing less than that we consider what a human being is. That is, we are led to consider how the specifically human manner of being is lit up, as it were, by man's interaction with his world through his hands. For this a new sort of anthropology is called for, one that is adequate to our experience of agency. Such an account might illuminate the appeal of manual work

> in a way that is neither romantic nor nostalgic, but rather simply gives credit to the practice of building things, fixing things, and routinely tending to things, as an element of human flourishing.[44]

What I offer isn't anthropology, but philosophy. And, I think, what analog offers to many is a feeling of being embodied and present in our own lives—something irreducibly contentful, and something inherent to feeling human.

Notes

1 Amazon, 'Lending for Kindle', *Amazon* (archived), n.d., https://web.archive.org/web/20140215095109/https://kdp.amazon.com/help?topicId=A2JGI9S4FDM39Q (accessed 7 March 2025); Barnes and Nobel, 'About NOOK LendMe Feature', *Barnes and Noble*, n.d., https://help.barnesandnoble.com/hc/en-us/articles/5447670380315-About-NOOK-LendMe-Feature (accessed 7 March 2025).

2 Reggie Ugwu, 'It's Their Content, You're Just Licensing It', *New York Times*, 4 April 2023, https://www.nytimes.com/2023/04/04/arts/dahl-christie-stine-kindle-edited.html (accessed 7 March 2025).

3 See Hannah Limerick, David Coyle, and James W. Moore (2014), 'The Experience of Agency in Human-Computer Interactions: A Review', *Frontiers in Human Neuroscience* 8: 1–10, at 4.

4 Wired, 'How Pinball Survived Video Games, the Mob and Politics,' *YouTube*, 18 April 2019, https://www.youtube.com/watch?v=VjrGMNEo7q0 (accessed 7 March 2025).

5 Barry Newman, 'In Short Supply: Pinball Wizards Who Can Fix Old Machines', *Wall Street Journal*, 7 September 2010, https://www.wsj.com/articles/SB10001424052748703882304575465613526210330 (accessed 7 March 2025).

6 Albert Borgmann (1984), *Technology and the Character of Contemporary Life: A Philosophical Inquiry* (Chicago: University of Chicago Press), 41.

7 James Howard Kunstler (2015), *A History of the Future* (New York: Grove Press), 10.

8 Ipsos MORI (2014), 'Global Trends 2014: Charting the New', *Ipsos*, https://www.ipsos.com/sites/default/files/ct/publication/documents/2020-01/ipsos-global-trends-2014-charts.pdf (accessed 7 March 2025).

9 Ipsos MORI (2021), 'Global Trends 2021: Aftershocks and Continuity', *Ipsos*, https://www.ipsos.com/sites/default/files/ct/publication/documents/2021-11/ipsos-global-trends-2021-report.pdf (accessed 7 March 2025).

10 Alex Vadukul, '"Luddite" Teens Don't Want Your Likes', *New York Times*, 15 December 2022, https://www.nytimes.com/2022/12/15/style/teens-social-media.html (accessed 7 March 2025).

11 Alex Vadukul, 'Now in College, Luddite Teens Still Don't Want Your Likes', 17 February 2025, https://www.nytimes.com/2025/01/30/style/luddite-teens-reunion.html (accessed 7 March 2025).

12 Lulu Garcia-Navarro, 'The Teenager Leading the Smartphone Liberation Movement', *First Person* (podcast), February 2 2023: https://www.nytimes.com/2023/02/02/opinion/teen-luddite-smartphones.html (accessed 7 March 2025).

13 Garcia-Navarro, 'The Teenager Leading'.

14 David Dupont, 'Teen Finds Power in Turning Off Smart Phone, Rejecting Social Media,' *BG Independent News*, 30 April 2024, https://bgindependentmedia.org/teen-finds-power-in-turning-off-smart-phone-rejecting-social-media/ (accessed 7 March 2025).

15 Vadukul, 'Now in College.'

16 Ralph Nader, 'Teenage iPhone Rebellion in Brooklyn', *CounterPunch*, 17 January 2023, https://www.counterpunch.org/2023/01/17/teenage-iphone-rebellion-in-brooklyn/ (accessed 7 March 2025).

17 Vadukul, 'Now in College.'

18 Nicolas Llasera, 'Adox Keynote || Film Foto Fair', *YouTube*, 25 March 2019, https://www.youtube.com/watch?v=G3bHwFlmBEY (accessed 7 March 2025).

19 Michael B. Beverland, Karen V. Fernandez, and Giana M. Eckhardt (2024), 'Consumer Work and Agency in the Analog Revival', *Journal of Consumer Research* 51, 719–738, at 726–727.

20 Bruno Berberian, Jean-Christophe Sarrazin, Patrick Le Blaye, and Patrick Haggard (2012), 'Automation Technology and Sense of Control: A Window on Human Agency', *PLoS One* 7(3): 1–6.

21 Beverland, Fernandez, and Eckhardt, 'Consumer Work and Agency in the Analog Revival', 733.

22 Adrienne Raphael, 'Why Adults Are Buying Coloring Books (for Themselves)', *New Yorker*, 12 July 2015, https://www.newyorker.com/business/currency/why-adults-are-buying-coloring-books-for-themselves (accessed 7 March 2025).

23 Raphael, 'Why Adults Are Buying Coloring Books'.

24 https://www.instagram.com/johannabasford/p/CvKYqcDos-O/ (accessed 7 March 2025).

25 Nielsen, 'Child's Play: Millennial Women Drive Sales of Adult Coloring Books', *Nielsen*, June 2016, https://www.nielsen.com/insights/2016/childs-play-millennial-women-drive-sales-of-adult-coloring-books/ (accessed 7 March 2025).

26 Amanda Diehl, 'On Trend: Adult Coloring Books', *Smart Bitches Trashy Books*, 8 December 2015, https://smartbitchestrashybooks.com/2015/12/trend-adult-coloring-books/ (accessed 7 March 2025).

27 Jordan Gaines Lewis, 'A Neuroscientist Patiently Explains the Allure of the Adult Coloring Book', *The Cut*, 10 January 2016, https://www.thecut.com/2016/01/neuroscientist-explains-adult-coloring-books.html (accessed 7 March 2025).

28 Sol LeWitt (1967), 'Paragraphs on Conceptual Art', *Artforum* 5(10), 79–83: 80.

29 Giorgio de Chirico (1971), 'The Return to the Craft', trans. Caroline Tisdall, in Massimo Carrà (ed), *Metaphysical Art*, 141–146 (New York: Praeger), at 143, 144–145.

30 R.G. Collingwood (1958), *Principles of Art* (Oxford: Oxford University Press), 133.

31 Mary Caroline Richards (1989), *Centering in Pottery, Poetry, and the Person*, 2nd Edn (Middletown, CT: Wesleyan University Press), 9.

32 Lambros Malafouris and Maria-Danae Koutouti (2022), 'Where the Touching is Touched: The Role of *Haptic Attentive Unity* in the Dialogue Between Maker and Material', *Multimodality & Society* 2(3), 265–287, at 267.

33 Tim Ingold (2013), *Making: Anthropology, Archaeology, Art and Architecture* (New York: Routledge), 101.

34 Anthony Cross (2024), 'Tool, Collaborator, or Participant: AI and Artistic Agency,' *British Journal of Aesthetics*, https://doi.org/10.1093/aesthj/ayae055, 4.

35 Cross, 'Tool, Collaborator, or Participant,' 4.

36 Erin O'Connor (2007), 'Embodied Knowledge in Glassblowing: The Experience of Meaning and the Struggle Towards Proficiency', *Sociological Review* 55(1 suppl.), 126–141, at 137.

37 SmartGirls Staff, 'Interview with Johanna Basford, Illustrator and Coloring Book Author', *Amy Poehler's Smart Girls*, 20 November 2015, https://amysmartgirls.com/interview-with-johanna-basford-illustrator-and-coloring-book-author-fc114dea8b48 (accessed 7 March 2025).

38 Lewis, 'A Neuroscientist Patiently Explains the Allure of the Adult Coloring Book'.

39 C. Thi Nguyen (2020), *Games: Agency as Art* (Oxford: Oxford University Press), 1.

40 Nguyen, *Games*, 18.

41 See, e.g. Sofia Bonicalzi (2024), 'Sense of Agency in Human-Human and Human-Computer Interactions,' in *Developments in Neuroethics* *and Bioethics*, Vol 7, ed. Marcello Ienca and Georg Starke, 85–100 (London: Academic Pres); Naho Saito, Keisue Takahata, Toshiya Murai, and Hidehiko Takahashi (2015), 'Discrepancy Between Explicit Judgement of Agency and Implicit Feeling of Agency: Implications for Sense of Agency and Its Disorders', *Consciousness and Cognition* 37, 1–7.

42 Anna Ciaunica, Luke McEllin, Julian Kiverstein, Vittorio Gallese, Jakob Hohwy & Mateusz Woźniak (2022), 'Zoomed Out: Digital Media Use and Depersonalization Experiences During the COVID-19 Lockdown', *Scientific Reports* 12, https://www.nature.com/articles/s41598-022-07657-8 (accessed 7 March 2025).

43 Anna Ciaunica, Julia Ayache, Patrick Haggard, Estelle Nakul, Emmanuelle Bonnet and Malika Auvray (2024), 'Explicit and Implicit Sense of Agency in Depersonalisation Experiences', *Scientific Reports* 14, https://doi.org/10.1038/s41598-024-65862-z (accessed 7 March 2025).

44 Matthew B. Crawford (2009), *Shop Class as Soulcraft: An Inquiry into the Value of Work* (New York: Penguin), 63–64.

5

Knowing What's Important

In the final episode of *Sex and the City*, Season 4, Carrie Bradshaw's love interest, Mr. Big, is packing to leave New York for Napa Valley. Carrie comes by the apartment, now mostly empty but for a few cardboard boxes. She digs into one and pulls out a vinyl record: "You kept nothing to sit on, but you have your records and a turntable?" she asks. "I know what's important," he replies.

When Delaina and I bought our house, two summers ago, we had to figure out how to put all of our stuff into a new space. Delaina and I have moved seven times since we got married 13 years ago, so this was not a *new* problem. But every move requires a new solution to that same problem. In particular, since our last move, we had accumulated hefty collections of vinyl records and board games, adding these to our already-large collections of books and comics.* When we first set out to shop

*Delaina also collects rocks. We have literal boxes of rocks stored in the house and shed. Anyone who burgles us will be sorely disappointed.

around for a house, we realized we needed one with an extra room just to contain all of that *stuff*. And now that we had it, we needed shelving. All of this would have been much easier (and, I'm sure, our house would have been cheaper) if all of our analog stuff had been digital instead. Digital stuff doesn't take up space. It doesn't require shelving—only more power outlets. But we had determined that all of this analog stuff was *important* enough for all of the hassle—important enough *for us*, at least.

Making choices often comes down to weighing values. When it comes to making medical choices, for example, your doctor will typically tend to prioritize physical longevity over other factors.[1] Of course, physicians are trained to preserve life where they can, and a value for duration of life tends to be embodied in that training. But patients sometimes weigh values differently, choosing *quality* of life over *quantity*—preferring the possibility of a shorter life that they can enjoy over the possibility of a longer life filled with suffering.[*] It's not that doctors don't recognize that their patients have complex value systems.[2] But medicine tends to treat duration of life as a sort of *objective* good. Everything else tends to get pretty subjective, pretty fast. How a given patient weighs, say, physical well-being versus psychological well-being versus financial security versus autonomy versus beauty will be impossible for any physician to predict. But if you think there *is* such a thing as an objective good, then you will tend to think that

[*] I have sleep apnea, and the doctor who diagnosed this suggested that I use a CPAP machine at night. I had used a CPAP in the sleep study used to diagnose me, and it was the worst night's sleep of my entire life. I accept that using a CPAP machine might extend my life, but a life with that kind of sleep is not a life I want more of.

this outweighs whatever subjective values it might be measured against—that it would be *irrational* to think otherwise. The driving principle of pragmatism, by contrast, suggests that there *are no* objective goods, that *every* value is ultimately subjective.

Technology—particularly *digital* technology—similarly tends to embrace efficiency and unencumbrance over everything else, treating these as objective goods. But *quality* of life can be found, too, in *inefficiency* and *encumbrance*. It can be found in richness of experience, in feeling oneself in one's own activities, and in engaging with individuals, whether those individuals are humans, plants, paper, cardboard, or vinyl. Writing this book has helped me to understand what it is that I value about analog, which seems so often at odds with efficiency and unencumbrance. And what I have discovered is that the values I find in analog are not specific to analog, but touch broad aspects of my life. This, too, is perfectly in keeping with the findings of pragmatism that started me off on this whole project. Our values aren't chunky, and aren't neatly compartmentalized. Rather, our values make up a broad web, stretching out over our lives and our daily activities. This makes it difficult at times to neatly separate our values for the sake of inquiry, or to separate those daily activities according to the values they engage with. As such, you might be forgiven for forgetting at various points that you were reading a book ostensibly about analog, thinking instead that you were reading a book about values more generally. Truthfully, I would forget, myself, on occasion.

The values I have focused on in this book—the value of material, the value of care, and the value of agency—tend to overlap in any number of ways, but without any one being subsumed by any other, and it has been a challenge to keep the inquiry organized in such a modular fashion: it tends to be at odds with how our values actually work. I could have as easily divided this book into chapters on the value of the individual, of presence, of experience and process. The field of values making up our lives is a messy thing, and so the line of inquiry running through this book has been anything but a straight line. I have tried to wander where my values led me. In the end, I have come to think of the values of analog as *grounding* values, as what calls us back to the hearth.

At the same time, none of this talk of the values of analog needs thus deny the values of the digital. I'm not writing this book on a typewriter, after all. Indeed, my writing process for the book began with an ongoing email thread with myself that I continually added to, hitting reply on my iPhone, and using voice-to-text to dictate whatever thought had just occurred to me. And although I have stacks of library books surrounding me, their pages filled with cascading sticky notes, I can't imagine how long it would have taken to do the research for this book without access to the Internet. Sometimes efficiency is *exactly* what I'm looking for.

When we moved into our new house, the layout of our new living room suggested something of an ideal arrangement of furniture, but that ideal arrangement itself presented a new issue. Between the obvious place for the large shelving unit for the records and turntable, and the speakers, which needed to be connected to the TV by fiber-optic cable, was an arched, frameless doorway. So, to connect the turntable by wire to the speakers required either an inelegant stringing of wire along the arched doorway, or else an *extremely* long wire the other way around, along three walls, and over the front door and fireplace. As such, I decided to go wireless. Now our turntable is connected to our speakers by Bluetooth. The analog signal from the turntable is converted by the Bluetooth transmitter into a digital signal, sent ten feet across the living room to the speakers, where the digital signal is then converted back to analog so we can hear Terry Snyder wailin' on the bongos. In this case, the value of agency that might have been found in stapling 100 feet of speaker wire around the baseboards, door frame, and fireplace, was beaten out by the value of efficiency embodied in Bluetooth technology (to say nothing of aesthetic value*). In truth, I felt my own agency in solving that problem and driving across town to pick up the Bluetooth transmitter that would get the job done.

While the analog *tends* to engage with and embody values distinct from those of the digital, they aren't mutually exclusive. I don't value the analog merely *because* it's unnecessarily difficult; I'm not a masochist. And none of the talk of the values of analog needs thus deny the values of the digital. This is not a zero-sum game. I can value both at the same time, even if they are at times in conflict with each other. Like the Bluetooth transmitter for my

---

*In the pursuit of efficiency, Jacques Ellul notes, "aesthetic considerations are gratuitous and permit the introduction of uselessness into an eminently useful and efficient apparatus." (*The Technological Society*, 73) Of course, something is "useless" if it doesn't help you pursue another end—and that's another way of saying that it's an end in itself.

turntable, there's a *lot* of technology designed so that you can analog the digital, and digital the analog: scanners for photos, printers for phones. Conversion allows us to move more fluidly between our values. Although the shine from new technology tends to be blinding, it also allows us an opportunity to reflect on what it was we valued in the old technology, usually without thinking about it.

The Turner-nominated artist Tacita Dean says, "I am attracted to obsolescence, so film is the perfect medium for me to work in."[3] "Obsolescence" is a strange concept—like a teleological death: the idea that something else better suits the end aimed at, effectively killing the old technology. Vinyl records are overtaken by cassette tapes, which are in turn overtaken by CDs.* Digital downloads overtake CDs, and are themselves overtaken by streaming. If we think of the end simply as access to music, then obsolescence ties in with efficiency. Similar stories could be told for photography, home video, books, games, and all manner of art and entertainment. But the resurgence of vinyl and all of these other forms of analog media suggests that, perhaps, there was some confusion about what the end was.

Perhaps Dean means that the *values* embodied in film photography are obsolete, but values don't tend to die out like that. Instead, they tend to sit quietly in the background until we find that something is missing in our lives. And, as our lives have grown increasingly digital, and especially as we experienced this in COVID lockdown, those values demanded our attention once

*8-tracks enjoy a brief moment in the lead of cassette tapes, but are an early casualty.

again. As Albert Borgmann suggests, "the simple things of yesterday attain a new splendor in today's technological context."[4] Borgmann writes, "[T]hose aspects or properties of a device that provide the answer to 'What is the device for?' constitute its commodity, and they remain relatively fixed."[5] As engineering gains new insights, the end stays fixed, and new devices compete as means to that end, to put the commodity in our hands. On this understanding, my turntable, and the iPad that I use to stream music to the same speakers, would seem to have the same commodity. But they don't. Rather, they are in service of different values.

For his part, Borgmann aims at a reform in the trajectory of technology: an about-face. I think he would have liked cozy post-apocalyptic novels. Unlike Borgmann, I don't think that technological trajectory is something that requires "reform"; rather, I think, relief is found in stepping to the side—getting off the highway, and exploring the backroads and towns along the way.

This book has been an exploration of its own. Anthony Weston suggested that if we want to know why he climbs mountains, it may take him hours to articulate "the manifold connections between mountain climbing and the other values, beliefs, etc. which make up my world," but it wouldn't be an *endless* task.[6] For my part, working through what it is that I value about analog took about 40,000 words. In the end, though, pragmatism suggests that values are about individuals. I can't tell you what you value, but I would suggest that it's probably worth giving it some thought.

Notes

1 Jay Katz (2002), *The Silent World of Doctor and Patient* (Baltimore, MD: Johns Hopkins University Press), 76.

2 See, e.g., Ariel Dempsey and John Mulder (2023), "Quality Versus Quantity of Life: Beyond the Dichotomy," *Palliative Medical Reports* 4(1): 17–23.

3 Christine Ross (2012), *The Past is the Present; It's the Future Too: The Temporal Turn in Contemporary Art* (London: Continuum), 166.

4 Albert Borgmann, *Technology and the Character of Contemporary Life*, 200.

5 Ibid., 43.

6 Anthony Weston (1987), 'Beyond Intrinsic Value: Pragmatism in Environmental Ethics', *Environmental Ethics* 7(4): 321–339, at 329.

Acknowledgments

Throughout this book, I've mentioned a lot of people who I've talked with about analog stuff while I've been thinking about what all of this stuff means to us. These conversations have been invaluable. Sam Martin and I chatted about aura and analog while we pulled weeds in the Sans Souci Community Garden. Ben Horne and I talked about Borgmann's focal things and practices while we sipped beers on my front porch. James Engelhardt and I talked about board games more times than I can count (about as many times as Laura Morris and I have talked about the books that surround us). Jared Stanley and I talked about printmaking over lunch at the Atlanta Bread Company, and Casey Parsons and I talked about the craft of painting on the Powerhouse patio. There is little that I haven't talked with Pete Groff and Maria Balcells about, from 8-tracks to comic books to mimeograph machines. Angela Black and I lamented the loss of agency when it comes to fixing our own cars, and Chris Alvin caught me up on the world of vintage game cartridge collectors. These people are my friends and neighbors, and I can't thank them enough for sharing their ideas, their expertise, and their lives. This wouldn't be the book it is without them.

Of course, throughout this book, you have heard a lot about my wife, Delaina. And how could you not? When I play board games, it's with her. When she finishes a good book, she passes it across the bed to me, and vice versa. When the record needs flipping, we take turns. How many hours have Delaina and I spent across the table from each other, putting together jigsaw puzzles, and searching the floor for missing pieces? And when those missing pieces can't be found, we have sat together at the firepit and watched those puzzles burn. As much as anything else, this book is the story of my life with Delaina, and every part of both the book and my life has been shaped by her. I can't imagine what either would have been without her, and I don't want to.

Several colleagues have provided support and feedback during the writing of this book, including Sarah Worth, whose office is next to mine and so is invariably drawn into conversation about whatever it is I'm thinking about on any given day, Brandon Polite, who flew me out to Knox College to give a talk on analog and lent me the use of his turntable, and Chris Bartel, who was the first person to read every word of this book, gave insightful feedback on every chapter, and took me and Delaina to the Asheville Pinball Museum. I know such great people.

Finally, my enormous thanks to Colleen Coalter, Senior Publisher of Philosophy at Bloomsbury Academic, who championed this project from the first time I suggested the idea to her at a diner in Arlington, Virginia. If I ask nicely, will you release an audiobook on cassette tape?

Bibliography

Adams, Zed (2018), 'Surface Noise', *British Journal of Aesthetics* 58(3), 255–270.

A La Maid (2021), 'Zen and the Art of Meditative Cleaning', *alamaid.com*, January 31, https://alamaid.com/zen-and-the-art-of-meditative-cleaning/

Alexander, Jennifer Karns (2008), *The Mantra of Efficiency: From Waterwheel to Social Contract* (Baltimore: Johns Hopkins University Press).

Amazon (n.d.), 'Lending for Kindle', *Amazon* (archived), https://web.archive.org/web/20140215095109/https://kdp.amazon.com/help?topicId=A2JGI9S4FDM39Q (accessed 7 March 2025).

Aristotle (1885), *Politics*, trans. B. Jowett (Oxford: Clarendon Press).

Aristotle (1980), *Nicomachean Ethics*, trans. David Ross (Oxford: Oxford University Press).

Aristotle (1987), 'Eudemian Ethics', trans. M. J. Woods, in *A New Aristotle Reader*, ed. J. L. Ackrill (Princeton, NJ: Princeton University Press).

Austin, James (2024), '5 Offline Games We Love for Camping (That Are Also Great for the Backyard)', *New York Times*, 3 June, https://www.nytimes.com/wirecutter/reviews/best-camping-backyard-games/ (accessed 7 March 2025).

Babauta, Leo (2012), "Mindful Simplicity: Decluttering, Cleaning & Leaving No Trace," *Zen Habits*, 4 September, https://zenhabits.net/mindful-simplicity/ (accessed 7 March 2025).

Baier, Annette C. (1995), *Moral Prejudices: Essays on Ethics* (Harvard University Press).

Barnes and Noble (n.d.), 'About NOOK LendMe Feature', *Barnes and Noble*, n.d., https://help.barnesandnoble.com/hc/en-us/

articles/5447670380315-About-NOOK-LendMe-Feature (accessed 7 March 2025).

Beard, Alison (2021), 'Life's Work: An Interview with Danielle Steel', *Harvard Business Review*, November-December, https://hbr.org/2021/11/lifes-work-an-interview-with-danielle-steel

Benjamin, Walter (1968), 'The Work of Art in the Age of Mechanical Reproduction', trans. Harry Zohn, in *Illuminations*, 219–253 (New York: Harcourt).

Berberian, Bruno, Jean-Christophe Sarrazin, Patrick Le Blaye, and Patrick Haggard (2012), 'Automation Technology and Sense of Control: A Window on Human Agency', *PLoS One* 7(3): 1–6.

Betancourt, Michael (2016), *The Critique of Digital Capitalism: An Analysis of the Political Economy of Digital Culture and Technology* (Santa Barbara, CA: Punctum Books).

Beverland, Michael B., Karen V. Fernandez, and Giana M. Eckhardt (2024), 'Consumer Work and Agency in the Analog Revival', *Journal of Consumer Research* 51, 719–738.

Binswanger, Julia (2024), 'This 4-Year-Old Shattered a Bronze Age Jar. Now, He'll Get to See How Experts Restored It', *Smithsonian Magazine*, 30 August, https://www.smithsonianmag.com/smart-news/this-4-year-old-shattered-a-bronze-age-jar-now-hell-get-to-see-how-experts-restored-it-180984999/ (accessed 7 March 2025).

Bonicalzi, Sofia (2024), 'Sense of Agency in Human-Human and Human-Computer Interactions', in *Developments in Neuroethics and Bioethics*, Vol 7, ed. Marcello Ienca and Georg Starke, 85–100 (London: Academic Press).

Borgmann, Albert (1984), *Technology and the Character of Contemporary Life: A Philosophical Inquiry* (Chicago: University of Chicago Press).

Bound Press (n.d.), "Kickstarter Campaign Announced for Nick Bantock, Griffin & Sabine App Trilogy', *PRWeb*, https://www.prweb.com/releases/kickstarter_campaign_announced_for_nick_bantock_griffin_sabine_app_trilogy/prweb12574897.htm (accessed 7 March 2025).

Candlin, Fiona (2010), *Art, Museums and Touch* (Manchester: Manchester University Press).

Caswell, Michelle, and Marika Cifor (2016), 'From Human Rights to Feminist Ethics: Radical Empathy in the Archives', *Archivaria* 81, 23–43.

Chackal, Tony (2025), 'Record Collecting as a Focal Practice: The Aesthetics and Sociality of Music Formats', *British Journal of Aesthetics*, https://doi.org/10.1093/aesthj/ayaf016.

Chad, Norman (2020), 'Being forced to play poker online serves as another reminder of why we need human contact', *Washington Post*, 19 April, https://www.washingtonpost.com/sports/being-forced-to-play-poker-online-serves-as-another-reminder-of-why-we-need-human-contact/2020/04/19/fb624a2c-8258-11ea-a3eb-e9fc93160703_story.html (accessed 7 March 2025).

Ciaunica, Anna, Julia Ayache, Patrick Haggard, Estelle Nakul, Emmanuelle Bonnet and Malika Auvray (2024), 'Explicit and Implicit Sense of Agency in Depersonalisation Experiences', *Scientific Reports* 14, https://doi.org/10.1038/s41598-024-65862-z (accessed 7 March 2025).

Ciaunica, Anna, Luke McEllin, Julian Kiverstein, Vittorio Gallese, Jakob Hohwy & Mateusz Woźniak (2022), 'Zoomed Out: Digital Media Use and Depersonalization Experiences During the COVID-19 Lockdown', *Scientific Reports* 12, https://www.nature.com/articles/s41598-022-07657-8 (accessed 7 March 2025).

Collingwood, R.G. (1958), *Principles of Art* (Oxford: Oxford University Press).

Crawford, Matthew B. (2009), *Shop Class as Soulcraft: An Inquiry into the Value of Work* (New York: Penguin).

Cross, Anthony (2024), 'Tool, Collaborator, or Participant: AI and Artistic Agency', *British Journal of Aesthetics*, https://doi.org/10.1093/aesthj/ayae055.

Curcic, Dimitrije (2023), 'Independent Bookstores Statistics', *WordsRated*, 10 February, https://wordsrated.com/independent-bookstores-statistics/ (accessed 7 March 2025).

Curzer, Howard J. (2007), 'Aristotle: Founder of the Ethics of Care', *Journal of Value Inquiry* 41, 221–243.

De Chirico, Giorgio (1971), 'The Return to the Craft', trans. Caroline Tisdall, in Massimo Carrà (ed), *Metaphysical Art*, 141–146 (New York: Praeger).

Dempsey, Ariel, and John Mulder (2023), "Quality Versus Quantity of Life: Beyond the Dichotomy," *Palliative Medical Reports* 4 (1): 17–23.

Dewey, John (1958), *Art as Experience* (New York: Capricorn Books).

Diehl, Amanda (2015), 'On Trend: Adult Coloring Books', *Smart Bitches Trashy Books*, 8 December, https://smartbitchestrashybooks.com/2015/12/trend-adult-coloring-books/ (accessed 7 March 2025).

Dupont, David (2024), 'Teen Finds Power in Turning Off Smart Phone, Rejecting Social Media', *BG Independent News*, 30 April, https://bgindependentmedia.org/teen-finds-power-in-turning-off-smart-phone-rejecting-social-media/ (accessed 7 March 2025).

Eede, Christian (2023), 'UK Vinyl Sales Increase for 16th Consecutive Year, With Over 5.9 million Sold in 2023', DJ, 20 December, https://djmag.com/news/uk-vinyl-sales-increase-16th-consecutive-year-over-59-million-sold-2023 (accessed 12 September 2025).

Eisler, Melissa (2017), 'Mindful Cleaning Practice: How to Wash, Sweep, and Fold with Presence', *Mindful Minutes*, March 30, https://mindfulminutes.com/mindful-cleaning-practice-wash-sweep-fold-presence/.

Ellul, Jacques (1964), *The Technological Society*, trans. John Wilkinson (New York: Knopf).

Ficino, Marsilio (1985), *Commentary on Plato's Symposium on Love*, trans. Sears Jayne (Dallas, TX: Spring Publications).

Field, Tiffany (2014), *Touch*, 2nd Edn (Cambridge, MA: MIT Press).

Gaines Lewis, Jordan Gaines (2016), 'A Neuroscientist Patiently Explains the Allure of the Adult Coloring Book', *The Cut*, 10 January, https://www.thecut.com/2016/01/neuroscientist-explains-adult-coloring-books.html (accessed 7 March 2025).

Garcia-Navarro, Lulu (2023), 'The Teenager Leading the Smartphone Liberation Movement', *First Person* (podcast), 2 February: https://www.nytimes.com/2023/02/02/opinion/teen-luddite-smartphones.html (accessed 7 March 2025).

Getsy, David J. (2011), 'Tactility or Opticality, Henry Moore or David Smith: Herbert Read and Clement Greenberg on *The Art of Sculpture*, 1956', *Anglo–American Exchange in Postwar Sculpture, 1945–1975*: https://www.getty.edu/museum/symposia/pdf_stark/stark_getsy.pdf (accessed 7 March 2025).

Goodman, Nelson (1976), *Languages of Art: An Approach to a Theory of Symbols*, 2nd Edn (Indianapolis: Hackett).

Hansen, Miriam Bratu (2008), 'Benjamin's Aura', *Critical Inquiry* 34(2), 336–375.

Hassan, Ahman, Chen Qibing, Jiang Tao, Lv Bing-Yang, Li Nian, Shu Li, Li Yu Tng, Ju Zhuo Li, Shang Guan Ziyue, and Muhammad Sohaib Tahir (2018), 'Effects of Plant Activity on Mental Stress in Young Adults', *HortScience* 53(1), 104–109.

Haugeland, John (1981), 'Analog and Analog', *Philosophical Topics* 12(1): 213–226.

Heritage Auctions (2024), 'Heritage Auctions Celebrates World's First $28+ Million Comics Auction', *Heritage Auctions*, 8 April, https://comics.ha.com/heritage-auctions-press-releases-and-news/heritage-auctions-celebrates-world-s-first-28-million-comics-auction.s?releaseId=4945 (accessed 7 March 2025).

Hill, Logan (2013), 'A Long Time Ago, in a Universe More Analog', *New York Times*, 27 October 2013, https://www.nytimes.com/2013/10/28/books/j-j-abrams-and-doug-dorst-collaborate-on-a-book-s.html (accessed 7 March 2025).

Holland, Oscar (2024), '4-year-old accidentally shatters Bronze Age jar at museum', *CNN*, 28 August, https://www.cnn.com/2024/08/28/style/israel-haifa-museum-boy-breaks-artifact-hnk-intl/index.html (accessed 7 March 2025).

Ingold, Tim (2013), *Making: Anthropology, Archaeology, Art and Architecture* (New York: Routledge).

Ipsos MORI (2014), 'Global Trends 2014: Charting the New', *Ipsos*, https://www.ipsos.com/sites/default/files/ct/publication/documents/2020-01/ipsos-global-trends-2014-charts.pdf (accessed 7 March 2025).

Ipsos MORI (2021), 'Global Trends 2021: Aftershocks and Continuity', *Ipsos*, https://www.ipsos.com/sites/default/files/ct/publication/documents/2021-11/ipsos-global-trends-2021-report.pdf (accessed 7 March 2025).

Irvin, Sherri (2008), 'The Pervasiveness of the Aesthetic in Ordinary Experience', *British Journal of Aesthetics* 48(1), 29–44.

Judah, Hettie (2024), '"Painting is a bodily activity": Hettie Judah on the more sensory pleasures of art', *Apollo* 199(730): 33–34.

Kania, Andrew (2006), 'Making Tracks: The Ontology of Rock Music', *Journal of Aesthetics and Art Criticism* 64(4), 401–414.

Kant, Immanuel (1987), *Critique of Judgment*, trans. Werner S. Pluhar (Indianapolis: Hackett).

Kant, Immanuel (2012), 'Lecture of the Winter Semester 1775–1776 based on the transcriptions Friedlander 3.3 (Ms 400), Friedlander 2

(Ms 399) and Prieger', trans. G. Felicitas Munzel, in *Lectures on Anthropology*, edited by Robert B. Louden, 43–256 (Cambridge University Press).

Katz, Jay (2002), *The Silent World of Doctor and Patient* (Baltimore: Johns Hopkins University Press).

Komar, Marlen (2019), 'Why touching art is so tempting – and exciting', *CNN*, 13 May 2019, https://www.cnn.com/style/article/why-we-want-to-touch-art/index.html (accessed 7 March 2025).

Konnikova, Maria (2020), *The Biggest Bluff* (New York: Penguin).

Kulvicki, John (2015), 'Analog Representation and the Parts Principle', *Review of Philosophy and Psychology* 6, 165–180.

Kulvicki, John (2017), 'Recording and Representing: Analog and Digital', in *Giving a Damn: Essays in Dialogue with John Haugeland*, edited by Zed Adams and Jacob Browning, 269–290 (Cambridge, MA: MIT Press).

Kunstler, James Howard (2015), *A History of the Future* (New York: Grove Press).

Lachs, Lorin (2025), 'Multi-Modal Perception', in *Noba Textbook Series: Psychology*, edited by R. Biswas-Diener and E. Diener (Champaign, IL: DEF).

Langer, Ellen J. and Judith Rodin (1976), 'The Effects of Choice and Enhanced Personal Responsibility for the Aged: A Field Experiment in an Institutional Setting', *Journal of Personality and Social Psychology* 34(2), 191–198.

Leathan, Tom (2023). 'Quentin Tarantino Explains Why He Shoots on Film', *Far Out*, 27 July, https://faroutmagazine.co.uk/why-quentin-tarantino-shoots-on-film/

Leddy, Thomas (2012), *The Extraordinary in the Ordinary* (Peterborough, ON: Broadview).

Leddy, Thomas (2018), 'The Aesthetics of Washing Dishes', *Aesthetics Today*, 4 May, https://aestheticstoday.blogspot.com/2018/05/the-aesthetics-of-washing-dishes.html (accessed 7 March 2025).

Lee, Min-sun, Juyoung Lee, Bum-Jin Park, and Yoshifumi Miyazaki (2015), 'Interaction with Indoor Plants May Reduce Psychological and Physiological Stress by Suppressing Autonomic Nervous System Activity in Young Adults: A Randomized Crossover Study', *Journal of Physiological Anthropology* 34(21). DOI 10.1186/s40101-014-0060-8.

Leu, Patrick (2024a), 'LP Album Unit Sales in the U.S. 1993-2023', *Statista*, 29 May, https://www.statista.com/statistics/188822/lp-album-sales-in-the-united-states-since-2009/ (accessed 7 March 2025).

Leu, Patrick (2024b), 'Physical Album Shipments in the U.S. 1999-2023', *Statista*, 7 June, https://www.statista.com/statistics/186772/album-shipments-in-the-us-music-industry-since-1999/ (accessed 7 March 2025).

Lewis, David (1971), 'Analog and Digital', *Noûs* 5(3): 321–327.

LeWitt, Sol (1967), 'Paragraphs on Conceptual Art', *Artforum* 5(10), 79–83.

Limerick, Hannah, David Coyle, and James W. Moore (2014), 'The Experience of Agency in Human-Computer Interactions: A Review', *Frontiers in Human Neuroscience* 8, 1–10.

Littleton, Harvey (1971), *Glassblowing: A Search for Form* (New York: Van Nostrand Reinhold).

Llasera, Nicolas (2019), 'Adox Keynote || Film Foto Fair', *YouTube*, 25 March, https://www.youtube.com/watch?v=G3bHwFlmBEY (accessed 7 March 2025).

Malafouris, Lambros, and Maria-Danae Koutouti (2022), 'Where the Touching is Touched: The Role of *Haptic Attentive Unity* in the Dialogue Between Maker and Material', *Multimodality & Society* 2(3), 265–287.

Malis, Nardi, Karina Fischer, Bess Dawson-Hughes, Endel J. Orav, Otto W. Meyer, Ursina Meyer, Sacha Beck, Hans-Peter Simmen, Hans-Christoph Pape, Andreas Egli, Walter C. Willett, Robert Theiler, and Heike A. Bischoff-Ferrari (2018), 'Association between Caregiver Role and Short- and Longer-Term Functional Recovery after Hip Fracture: A Prospective Study', *JAMDA* 19, 122–129.

Martin, Daniel, Sandra Malpica, Diego Gutierrez, Belen Masia, and Ana Serrano (2022), 'Multimodality in VR: A Survey', *AMC Computing Surveys* 54(10s): 216:1–216:36.

Matthes, Erich Hatala (2024), *What to Save and Why: Identity, Authenticity, and the Ethics of Conservation* (Oxford: Oxford University Press).

Medley, Mark (2016), 'Nick Bantock on the End of Griffin and Sabine's Epic Correspondence', *Globe and Mail*, 25 March, https://www.theglobeandmail.com/arts/art-and-architecture/griffin-and-sabine-creator-nick-bantock-on-the-end-of-an-epic-correspondence/article29391999/ (accessed 7 March 2025)

Menabrea, Luigi Federico (1843), 'Sketch of the Analytical Engine Invented by Charles Babbage, Esq', trans. with notes by Ada Lovelace, *Scientific Memoirs* 3: 666–731.

Mezil, Ahmen (2023), 'The Art of Mindful Cleaning: Cleaning with Intention and Awareness', *Hellamaid*, 10 May, https://hellamaid.ca/mental-health/the-art-of-mindful-cleaning-cleaning-with-intention-and-awareness/

Miller, John P. (2019), *The Holistic Curriculum*, 3rd Edn (University of Toronto Press).

Mitchell, E.T. (1945), 'Dewey's Theory of Valuation', *Ethics* 55(4): 287–297.

Nader, Ralph (2023), 'Teenage iPhone Rebellion in Brooklyn', *CounterPunch*, 17 January, https://www.counterpunch.org/2023/01/17/teenage-iphone-rebellion-in-brooklyn/ (accessed 7 March 2025).

National Institutes of Health (2024), 'Caring for Yourself while Caring for Others', *MedlinePlus*, 5 November, https://magazine.medlineplus.gov/article/caring-for-yourself-while-caring-for-others

Newman, Barry (2010), 'In Short Supply: Pinball Wizards Who Can Fix Old Machines', *Wall Street Journal*, 7 September, https://www.wsj.com/articles/SB10001424052748703882304575465613526210330 (accessed 7 March 2025).

Nguyen, C. Thi (2020), *Games: Agency as Art* (Oxford: Oxford University Press).

Nguyen, C. Thi, and Bekka Williams (2020), 'Moral Outrage Porn', *Journal of Ethics and Social Philosophy* 18(2): 147–172.

Nguyen, C. Thi, and Bekka Williams (2019), 'Why We Call Things "Porn"', *New York Times*, 26 July, https://www.nytimes.com/2019/07/26/opinion/sunday/porn.html (accessed 7 March 2025).

Nielsen (2016), 'Child's Play: Millennial Women Drive Sales of Adult Coloring Books', *Nielsen*, June, https://www.nielsen.com/insights/2016/childs-play-millennial-women-drive-sales-of-adult-coloring-books/ (accessed 7 March 2025).

Noddings, Nel (1984), *Caring: A Feminine Approach to Ethics & Moral Education* (Berkeley, CA: University of California Press).

O'Connor, Erin (2007), 'Embodied Knowledge in Glassblowing: The Experience of Meaning and the Struggle Towards Proficiency', *Sociological Review* 55(1 suppl.), 126–141.

Oldenburg, Ray (1999), *The Great Good Place* (New York: Marlowe & Company).

Peterson, Grant (2012), *Just Ride: A Radically Practical Guide to Riding Your Bike* (New York: Workman).

Pirsig, Robert M. (1999), *Zen and the Art of Motorcycle Maintenance: An Inquiry into Values* (New York: William Morrow & Co.).

Plato (1963), *Greater Hippias*, in *The Collected Dialogues of Plato Including the Letters*, trans. Benjamin Jowett, ed. Edith Hamilton and Huntington Cairns (Princeton, NJ: Princeton University Press).

Plato (1992), *Republic*, trans. G.M.A. Grube (Indianapolis: Hackett).

Polite, Brandon, and Aaron Meskin (2025), 'Why Record Shops Matter Aesthetically: A Case Study in Aesthetic Institutions', *Journal of Aesthetics and Art Criticism* 83(2): 165–176.

Polite, Brandon, and Elizabeth Scarbrough (2025), 'Patina of Sound: Valuing Vinyl Records as Relics of Aged Interaction', *Espes* 14(1): 104–122.

Purkis, Jon (2020), 'Top 10 Board Games to Play on Tabletop Simulator', *YouTube*, 23 April, https://www.youtube.com/watch?v=JasuCclZ1v0 (accessed 7 March 2025).

Raphael, Adrienne (2015), 'Why Adults Are Buying Coloring Books (for Themselves)', *New Yorker*, 12 July, https://www.newyorker.com/business/currency/why-adults-are-buying-coloring-books-for-themselves (accessed 7 March 2025).

Rea, Michael C. (2001), 'What Is Pornography?' *Noûs* 35(1): 118–145.

Read, Herbert (1956), *The Art of Sculpture* (New York: Pantheon Books).

Richards, Mary Caroline (1989), *Centering in Pottery, Poetry, and the Person*, 2nd Edn (Middletown, CT: Wesleyan University Press).

Richter, Felix (2024), 'Despite Comeback, Vinyl Is Still Far From Its Glory Days', *Statista*, 19 April, https://www.statista.com/chart/7699/lp-sales-in-the-united-states/ (accessed 7 March 2025).

Riegl, Alois (1996), 'The Modern Cult of Monuments: Its Essence and Its Development', trans. Karin Bruckner and Karen Williams, in Nicholas Stanley-Price, Mansfield Kirby Talley, and Alesandra Melucco Vaccaro, Alessandra, *Historical and Philosophical Issues in the Conservation of Cultural Heritage*, 69–83 (Los Angeles: Getty Conservation Institute).

Ronin, Judith, and Ellen J. Langer (1977), 'Long-Term Effects of a Control-Relevant Intervention with the Institutionalized Aged', *Journal of Personality and Social Psychology* 35(12), 897–902.

Rosenblatt, Bill (2023), 'Luminate Data Music Report: The Album Is Once Again a Vinyl LP', *Forbes*, 24 May. https://www.forbes.com/sites/

billrosenblatt/2023/01/16/luminate-data-music-report-the-album-is-once-again-a-vinyl-lp/ (accessed 7 March 2025).

Ross, Brenda (2016), 'Griffin and Sabine by Nick Bantock', *Info Cafe*, 20 October 2016, https://blogs.davenportlibrary.com/reference/griffin-and-sabine-by-nick-bantock/ (accessed 7 March 2025).

Saito, Naho, Keisue Takahata, Toshiya Murai, and Hidehiko Takahashi (2015), 'Discrepancy Between Explicit Judgement of Agency and Implicit Feeling of Agency: Implications for Sense of Agency and Its Disorders', *Consciousness and Cognition* 37, 1–7.

Saito, Yuriko (2007), *Everyday Aesthetics* (Oxford: Oxford University Press).

Saito, Yuriko (2017), *The Aesthetics of the Familiar: Everyday Life and World-Making* (Oxford: Oxford University Press).

Saito, Yuriko (2022), *Aesthetics of Care: Practice in Everyday Life* (London: Bloomsbury).

Sax, David (2016), *The Revenge of Analog: Real Things and Why They Matter* (New York: PublicAffairs).

Sax, Joseph L. (1999), *Playing Darts with a Rembrandt: Public and Private Rights in Cultural Treasures* (Ann Arbor, MI: University of Michigan Press).

Schmitz, Rob (2020), 'Sales Of "Settlers Of Catan" Skyrocket During Coronavirus Crisis', *NPR*, 4 August, https://www.npr.org/2020/08/04/898853332/sales-of-settlers-of-catan-skyrocket-during-coronavirus-crisis (accessed 7 March 2025).

Schwartz, Barry (2004), *The Paradox of Choice: Why More Is Less* (New York: HarperCollins).

Sega of America (1976) Promotional Brochure. https://www.pinrepair.com/arcade/fonz.htm (accessed 7 March 2025).

Shaftesbury [Sir Anthony Ashley Cooper] (1999), *The Moralists*, in *Characteristics of Men, Manners, Opinions, Times*, 231–338 (University of Cambridge Press).

Shiner, Larry (2012), '"Blurred Boundaries'? Rethinking the Concept of Craft and its Relation to Art and Design', *Philosophy Compass* 7/4, 230–244.

Slepian, Michael L., Steven G. Young, Abraham M. Rutchick, and Nalini Ambady (2013), 'Quality of Professional Players' Poker Hands Is Perceived Accurately from Arm Motions', *Psychological Science* 24(11), 2335–2338.

SmartGirls Staff (2015), 'Interview with Johanna Basford, Illustrator and Coloring Book Author', *Amy Poehler's Smart Girls*, 20 November, https://amysmartgirls.com/interview-with-johanna-basford-illustrator-and-coloring-book-author-fc114dea8b48 (accessed 7 March 2025).

Statista (2005), 'Board Games – Worldwide', *Statista*, January, https://www.statista.com/outlook/cmo/toys-hobby/toys-games/board-games/worldwide (accessed 7 March 2025).

Tavinor, Grant (2021), *Aesthetics of Virtual Reality* (New York: Routledge).

Taylor Corporation (2025), 'The Vinyl Record Industry: Why Is There a Resurgence of Vinyl Records?', *Taylor.com*, August 5, https://www.taylor.com/blog/increased-vinyl-sales-and-the-vinyl-revival (accessed 12 September 2025).

Tighe, D. (2024), 'Board Games Market Value Worldwide from 2017 to 2023', *Statista*, 22 February. https://www.statista.com/statistics/829285/global-board-games-market-value/ (accessed 7 March 2025).

Tingen, Paul (2014), 'Inside Track: Jack White', *Sound on Sound*, October, https://www.soundonsound.com/techniques/inside-track-jack-white

Tingen, Paul (2021), 'Paul Tingen: Taylor Swift "willow"', *Sound on Sound*, March, https://www.soundonsound.com/techniques/inside-track-taylor-swift-willow

Ucar, Ezgi (2015), 'Multisensory Met: Touch, Smell, and Hear Art', The Met, 8 September, https://www.metmuseum.org/articles/multisensory-met (accessed 7 March 2025).

Ugwu, Reggie (2023), 'It's Their Content, You're Just Licensing It', *New York Times*, 4 April, https://www.nytimes.com/2023/04/04/arts/dahl-christie-stine-kindle-edited.html (accessed 7 March 2025).

Vadukul, Alex (2022), '"Luddite" Teens Don't Want Your Likes', *New York Times*, 15 December, https://www.nytimes.com/2022/12/15/style/teens-social-media.html (accessed 7 March 2025).

Vadukul, Alex (2025), 'Now in College, Luddite Teens Still Don't Want Your Likes', 17 February, https://www.nytimes.com/2025/01/30/style/luddite-teens-reunion.html (accessed 7 March 2025).

Weston, Anthony (1987), 'Beyond Intrinsic Value: Pragmatism in Environmental Ethics', *Environmental Ethics* 7(4): 321–339.

Wired (2019), 'How Pinball Survived Video Games, the Mob and Politics', *YouTube*, 18 April, https://www.youtube.com/watch?v=VjrGMNEo7q0 (accessed 7 March 2025).

Worth, Sarah E. (2021), *Taste: A Philosophy of Food* (London: Reaktion Books).

Index